S.U.C.C.E.S.S.

Create Your Own Pathway

DEBBIE JACOBSON, PH.D.

BALBOA.
PRESS
A DIVISION OF HAY HOUSE

Balboa Press books may be ordered through booksellers or by contacting:

Balboa Press
A Division of Hay House
1663 Liberty Drive
Bloomington, IN 47403
www.balboapress.com
1 (877) 407-4847

Because of the dynamic nature of the Internet, any web addresses or links contained in this book may have changed since publication and may no longer be valid. The views expressed in this work are solely those of the author and do not necessarily reflect the views of the publisher, and the publisher hereby disclaims any responsibility for them.

The author of this book does not dispense medical advice or prescribe the use of any technique as a form of treatment for physical, emotional, or medical problems without the advice of a physician, either directly or indirectly. The intent of the author is only to offer information of a general nature to help you in your quest for emotional and spiritual well-being. In the event you use any of the information in this book for yourself, which is your constitutional right, the author and the publisher assume no responsibility for your actions.

Any people depicted in stock imagery provided by Thinkstock are models, and such images are being used for illustrative purposes only.
Certain stock imagery © Thinkstock.

ISBN: 978-1-4525-2012-4 (sc)
ISBN: 978-1-4525-2013-1 (e)

Printed in the United States of America.

Balboa Press rev. date: 10/09/2014

DEDICATION

I dedicate this book to my husband, Eric, who has lovingly stood by me through all my growing-up pains. You were meant for me.

This book is also dedicated to my clients, those whose stories I used in this book and all the others. Thank you all for helping me grow and learn.

ACKNOWLEDGMENTS

To Nadine Gross - We met by chance, but you have changed my life. Without meeting you, there would be no book. It was all in my star chart. Thank you.

To Marlene Cobb - You have been my mentor since the day we met. Your knowledge about healing, acupuncture, NET, NAET and intuitive abilities are a constant amazement to me. I want to be just like you.

To Larry Dolinsky - You started as our therapist and become a dear friend. You met us while we were in the depths of confusion and despair at a time in our lives when we were weakened by loss and tragedy. You taught us more about life and our love for each other than I ever knew possible. Thank you for showing me the ease of rewriting my life's story.

To Linda, Jim, Grace, Carolina, Steve, Shantelle, Wendy, Lynda, Terry, Val, Kelly and Arron: You are dear friends who have helped me open my mind and cheered me on every step of the way. I have been blessed with the most caring and loving community of friends. We are so blessed to have found each other and we know it. You have taught me about success.

For my beautiful daughter Barbara and my granddaughters Xoe and Xamara~ you added joy and love into my heart! Love you forever!

Special thanks once again to my technology guru Jim Barber! He makes the impossible easy and just kind of shrugs when I gush with appreciation.

Also heartfelt thanks to Arron Haggart with the photographer's heart who can do anything with images!

Wishing everyone everywhere around this beautiful planet laughter and tons of butterfly kisses!

CONTENTS

ON A PERSONAL NOTE- A BIT ABOUT ME

Since we are going on a journey together of looking inward and making positive changes, I thought you might like to know a bit about me. I won't bore you, but I prefer to connect with an author, and if you agree, you'll read this page. If you don't, or are just feeling ornery today, skip ahead, read out of order, do what you feel you need to do. Personally, I love to read the whole book, cover to cover, but that's just me.

I guess I've always felt different from other people. I was never one to make small talk at a party. Everyone else seemed so good at it, and they seemed so comfortable. I fidgeted, felt out of place, and really wanted to go home. So I tried and tried and kept on trying, always feeling like an outsider and definitely not feeling successful. Oh believe me, I longed to "be like everybody else" but it wasn't meant to be for me.

Years went by and I soon realized there were lots of other people who felt as different as I did. I went back to school to learn more, and now I work with others as a Life Transformation Coach and Holistic Nutritionist. These are ordinary people who are ready to grow and be more successful in their lives. You will read about some of my clients. The names are all made up. I have kept them anonymous because their life experiences on the road to success are the most important part.

As I got older, and worked on myself through positive affirmations, therapy, and meditation, I am now working on totally and completely accepting myself for who I am and who I will be. As a lifelong learner, I know the journey is never over and I appreciate everything and express gratitude for all of my life experiences. So here is the bottom line.

I am not perfect. I am oh so not perfect, but that's okay. I'm me. I am who I am. I am. My wish for you is that you feel the same exact way about yourself!

HOW TO USE THIS BOOK

Of course you can use this book any way that works best for you, but I'd like to make a few suggestions.

First of all, I would suggest you buy a notebook or journal for use with this book. You will find exercises throughout the book that will request you to think about and respond in writing. You will want to revisit those pages and update them on a pretty regular basis.

I keep my notebooks and refer back to them over the years. I jot down interesting items: affirmations, snippets of articles from magazines and newspapers. I collect cards, thank you notes, words of wisdom as I come across them and of course pictures and photos. I like to draw, list, decorate, and notate all over the pages.

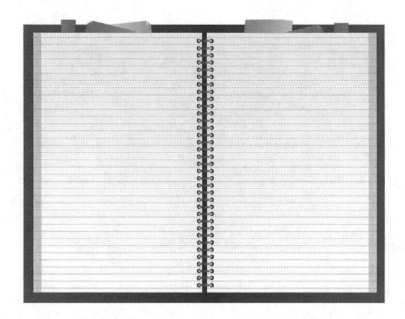

Also, I love to read with a pen in my hand. I write in the margins, underline important words or phrases, and generally interact with what I am reading. I make connections to my past and present life. I also connect with the text, the author, and the words on the page. Some of my best thoughts and ideas have been triggered by minds greater than I could ever imagine.

REASONS WHY I KEEP A JOURNAL, SHOULD YOU?

I have always loved the feel and smell of new notebooks, pens, pencils, crayons—anything that comes from an office supply store. I own every color highlighter, both fine point and bullet tip. I am gaga for different shapes, sizes and colors of Post-it notes too. I wish I had invented them. The best part of back to school every year was carefully choosing the "bestest" of everything I would need for writing. I guess I was born with a story, or two, or many, in my head. The smell of a new blank black and white composition notebook expanded my heart to the edge of ecstasy. (I know-cheap date, right?)

I have so many journals; they fit in piles in drawers. They are messy, tabbed with all kinds of Post-it notes, tattered and worn pieces of paper and magazine clippings that stick out of the edge of the journal a bit too much. I am not a person who likes clutter, however I collect words and ideas and feelings and save them forever in between the pages of my journals. Some are fancy leather-bound (gifts probably) and other are simple 70 page spirals. But when I open one of them and sit on the floor cozy with my journals, I transcend space and time. I travel vicariously through the stars and escape the mortal realm.

So here is my list: <u>Top Nine Reasons Why I Keep A Journal</u>

9. A safe place to figure things out. Sometimes I ask what others think, but I prefer to go within and rely on what my intuition tells me. That is something I have learned. I always used to second guess myself. Through meditation, I have finally figured out how and when to listen to my personal navigation system, AKA my gut feeling.

8. Focus – uh yeah! When I have so many roles to play my mind just flits from one topic to another. Sometimes writing down a thought in my journal is the first time I actually decipher new ideas or thoughts without having to say them aloud and possibly be judged. Journaling may go off on a tangent here and there but for the most part exploring my own thinking and ideas on paper works to focus me.

7. A journal is a fabulous place to just let go-anger, anxiety, frustration, a clever comeback that hit you after the other person walked away. This is a place where I let go with the dirty, ugly and maybe even inappropriate. I also write down lessons I've learned. I am not the manager of the Universe and in my journals, I give myself permission to let go of being in control of everything and/or everyone. It is a stress buster! Most of the best lessons I've learned have come from difficult moments, but I learn, scrape off the bottom of my shoe, and keep walking!

6. This book is all about success-what better way to track your successes and accomplishments step-by-step? I have been able to achieve some things in my life that I never thought possible. I went back to school to study for a doctorate at age 50. It took me several years to finish, but I did it!

5. What a terrific stress reducer! Writing down my thoughts, feelings and desires helps me get things straight in my head. I feel the stress subside as the pen rolls across line after line. Breakthrough understandings of other people or situations can come through journaling too. Suddenly you can understand others or something that happened with new eyes.

4. Ever get an idea-seems a little out there, too crazy to say aloud? This is the perfect place to let your creativity flow. Write down your ideas; give them time to brew and possibly even hatch. The top of that list in my journal is called "Freakin' Awesome Ideas". If I talked about them people might get worried about my sanity, but I know there is something good brewing.

3. As you set off to create your pathway to success, you will no doubt increase your self-awareness. My journal holds snippets of language and quotes that inspire me. I have learned how to meditate and go within. I have learned how to listen to my inner voice. These were things that used to seem too "woo woo" for me. You will recognize your Super Powers!

2. An amazing benefit of journaling is becoming a witness to your own spiritual and emotional healing and growth. I was once an angry person with little to no self-esteem. When I read back through my journals, I hardly recognize who that person was and at the same time I am filled with gratitude for how far I've come. I recently rewrote my resume which hadn't been updated for a decade. I was impressed! I would definitely hire me!

1. I remember the first time I heard the name Louise Hay and the power of affirmations. My life changed as I read her books, watched her on YouTube and in movies. More than just positive thinking, affirmations help set your intentions

so you can accomplish your goals. I love to make up my own affirmations or use hers. Either way, write them in your journal, on mirrors, on little pieces of paper you stick in your pocket and sticky notes on the steering wheel of your car! I have done and still do all of the above! I also receive a daily free email from www.tut.com which is an uplifting message. I print them out, paste them in my journal and write about my feelings toward the words.

Those are just a few of the reasons I journal. If you have never tried it, go ahead. Buy a great notebook and pens that tickle your fancy. If you have journaled in the past but didn't stick with it, I would recommend you try again. If you feel more comfortable, start with a Gratitude Journal. Once, during a dark time in my life, I would force myself to come up with five entries for each day. Suddenly, I began to see all the wonderful things, people and situations in my life to be grateful for. Now I stop myself hundreds of time each day and just close my eyes for an instant and acknowledge as many blessings as I can. A grateful heart is a happy heart. Happy hearted people sleep well at night and smile for no reason during the day. Wouldn't you want to hang out with people like that?

WHAT MAKES PEOPLE SUCCEED?

You already know deep inside why you haven't made all your wishes and dreams come true, because the answer is always inside. Your emotional brain will tell you, "You're crazy! Who do you think you are?" or something like, "That only happens to other people. You don't deserve it!" This nagging, negative voice is always lurking in the background. It believes it is keeping you safe, but in reality it holds you back from being your best.

So you think other people have all the luck and you just missed out? Are you tired of trying one foolproof plan after another and feeling like a fool? Has your negative, nagging voice taken over? You know the one. It tells you, "You can't. Don't even try. You don't deserve it."

Pull up a seat and get comfortable. You have picked up the right book to start bringing success into your life today!

People fail for many reasons, but fear is underlying most of them. We learn over our lifetimes to be afraid and in some instances that works well for us. However, when fear takes over and controls our thoughts and actions, we tend to increase our failure to success ratio. We begin to act and think based on emotions stored in the limbic part of the brain, which may not even be based on reality. Historical reality and emotional reality may not match, but if we feel something is real, our brain perceives it that way.

Failing does not feel good. We don't want to keep doing it. We love the feeling of success. We are elated, flying high, and we want to do it again and again. Know what? We can convince ourselves of failure simply by believing it, and holding on to that belief so tightly that we are not aware we are doing so. We can create a physical response in the body simply by accepting and dwelling on this belief.

Franklin Delano Roosevelt is famous for his words about fear during his first inaugural address. However, the words we are all so familiar with are only a part of the sentence. Here it is in its entirety: "So, first of all, let me assert my firm belief that the only thing we have to fear is fear itself – nameless, unreasoning, unjustified terror which paralyzes needed efforts to convert retreat into advance."

The man was talking about our country's involvement in World War II, but what about the battle raging inside all of us? We fight a war every day with our very own thoughts. We all have a nagging, negative voice bringing us down, crushing our confidence and boldness. The fear he mentions is the same fear you face: "…the nameless, unreasoning, unjustified terror which paralyzes needed efforts to convert retreat into advance."

That confidence, that ability to face your terrors is what sets you on your mission to create your own pathway to success. Fear is nameless. We aren't sure from where it springs, but we feel it. Your boss asks you to present to a prospective client and the feeling of terror is palpable, running up and down your spine. That nagging, negative voice starts buzzing and you do feel paralyzed.

The fear of public speaking is the most common fear in America. However, it is inexorably enmeshed with leadership, motivation and change.

How can you convert your retreat into advance? Mahatma Gandhi said, "True morality consists not in following the beaten track, but in finding the true path for ourselves, and fearlessly following it." This is your opportunity to write the rest of your life story the way you want it to be. This is your opportunity to create your own pathway to success. This book will help you find your own way.

Would we be able to convince ourselves equally of success simply by believing it and accepting it? You bet! That is why I wrote this book. I have personally changed my beliefs, over a period of time, and changed my life too. I went from being a mostly negative person, to a person who is positive more often than not. I expect success, believe in my ability to attain it, and time after time, it comes to pass. I was wired from my childhood to be a negative thinker and expect the worst, and so I was and the worst happened, many times.

I was able to change that wiring with a dedication to wanting more for myself. I want to be happy and enjoy my life. Every year for my birthday I choose something positive to focus on and spend the year concentrating on bringing it into my life. One year my quest was to find the joy in my life. What a great year that was! Life has been so much more fun since then too.

When you feel like a failure, when you're down on yourself, the whole world seems bleak. It is so hard to feel the sun on your face and crack a smile. If you keep this going for any period of time, you are not fun to be around, and you just add loneliness onto the pile of all the things wrong with your life. You know the saying, "Chalk it up to experience." You start to internalize it as, "Chalk it up to another failure." Gloomy Gus. Negative Nellie. You don't even enjoy your own company.

What are feelings anyway? Simply, feelings are energy. It is the energy of your feelings that creates a positive or negative spin on what you think and believe, and can even effect your health. You have heard the saying like attracts like, and it is true. Called the Law of Attraction, the energy of your thoughts will attract more into your life. If the energy is positive, more will flow to you. Unfortunately, it works both ways.

"Stop being afraid of what could go wrong
And start being positive of what could go right."
~Unknown

Dale Carnegie said, "You can conquer almost any fear if you will only make up your mind to do so. For remember, fear doesn't exist anywhere except in the mind." Fear is something you do to yourself by having fearful thoughts and/or expectations. The feelings of fear will restrict you in every way; what you think, what you do, and what you say. Sometimes you might be aware that a fear is not real, maybe even irrational or ridiculous. But the reactions created in both your physical body and your emotional self is real. Fear is not logical. It is not a thing. It is simply a response, both physical and emotional/mental, to what you anticipate may (or may not) happen.

Fear is learned. Fears are developed by your past experiences and the past experiences of others. Your reaction to the fear is what paralyzes you or thrusts you forward with confidence and strength. Using your failures as a learning opportunity helps you develop a trust in yourself and create the life you want.

Have you seen the movie "The Secret" or read the book? If not, you should. This is a great starting point to understand the Law of Attraction. It is a documentary type of movie consisting of a series of interviews explaining that your thoughts and feelings can attract into your life what you want. The Law of Attraction has two parts: (1) like attracts like and (2) what you focus on causes expansion. If you are happy and positive, you will attract more of that into your life. Remember, what you think about becomes your intentions. By focusing on something you can make it happen. The more you focus, the more powerful it becomes. You create your own reality by focusing your thoughts on what it is you want. That is exactly how you can create your own pathway to success.

Generally, Americans are over-thinkers. We think we need time to think things through, to sleep on it and get back to someone. Some people, I hope you aren't one of them, can become paralyzed by their indecisiveness. Have you learned over time to ignore your gut feeling, your innate intuition, and focus on rationalizing and reasoning? You are not alone. It's part of our American culture.

Your thoughts are energy. Energy vibrates and moves. The quality of your life as it is right now is the result of your previous thoughts. Happy? Keep doing what you have been doing. Not so much? Then now is the time to make some changes. The only person on the planet who can change you, is YOU. So, get ready to see the world with new eyes thinking new thoughts. You can create a future that will unfold according to your vision of it. No matter what is going on in the present moment, be assured you can attract what you desire, and quickly. You are ready, let's begin.

YOUR BRAIN

"I do not think there is any thrill that can go through the human heart
like that felt by the inventor
as he sees some creation of the brain unfolding to success..."
~Nikola Tesla

Your brain is marvelous and wondrous and without it life ceases to exist. What does your brain have to do with success? With fears? With a lack of confidence? In a word- everything!

Most of us know that the brain is divided into two hemispheres. These parts of the brain are generally referred to as left brain and right brain. It is scientific and easy for all to understand. The left brain hemisphere is logical, orderly, the scientist and mathematician in you. This hemisphere thinks linearly, analytically, is realistic and practical. If you have been reading this and thinking "I must have missed that line when they were handing out the brains," then let's talk about the right hemisphere. Think art, poetry, movement, color. This side of the brain feels and senses, imagines and creates.

The two hemispheres, although seemingly so different, are highly complementary. In fact the left brain controls the right side of your body and vice versa. There are literally thousands of chemical reactions happening in your brain every second. Don't you feel smarter already? Men and women do have different structures and wiring in their brains. The frontal lobe, which is responsible for decision making and problem solving, as well as the limbic cortex, which regulates emotion, are more highly developed in women than in men.

In actuality your brain weighs about 3 pounds and is soft and has the consistency of tofu. It is mostly made up of water (about 75%) and fat (the reason you keep hearing about the need for quality healthy oils-it feeds the brain). While in utero, the brain takes the longest of all organs to develop. It also goes through more changes. Some scientists believe that the human brain is the most mysterious thing in the entire cosmos.

Your brain is so marvelous and wondrous, in fact, that you have THREE brains! They are all in one spot in your skull, but they function differently for different reasons. The Reptilian Brain, the Neocortex Brain, and the Mammalian Brain are what control and drive your existence. These three components work together.

The Reptilian Brain is mostly unconscious, and is driven by the most basic needs of feeding, fear and flight or fight. I like to think of it as the four Fs. This brain is all about your survival. You don't need to remind your heart to beat, or your lungs to breathe. Your Reptilian Brain controls body temperature, heart rate, and balance which automatically take place in the Reptilian Brain. You probably learned about the fight vs. flight mechanism in science class. It is the most primitive and designed to protect you and keep you safe. It is instinctual.

The Neocortex Brain is mostly conscious. This part of your brain is what we referred to above; the two hemispheres, left and right brain. This is where decision making takes place, you reason, compose, do math, understand, and invent. The good news is that this part of the brain is flexible and has almost infinite learning abilities. Psychologists believe that we are 80% non-conscious of our motivations and behaviors. This brain would love to take over and be in total control all the time. It will fight you for power.

Are you wondering why in the world you are reading about the brain? Do you think you have the wrong book? Hold on. We are getting to the most important brain, the Mammalian Brain. This brain is mostly subconscious. This is the part of the brain where emotions and memory of them are formed and stored. The Mammalian Brain is less an organ of thought and more of an organ of feeling.

What does any of this have to do with a book about creating a pathway to success? What are your childhood memories of family? Do you feel your current level of education facilitates your success at work? Are you feeling well financially? What about your relationships? If any, all, or a combination of the above have had an effect on your lack of success, it possibly is connected to memories stored in the limbic part of the Mammalian Brain.

I don't want to confuse you. I do want you to understand that the past has definite underpinnings on the decisions you make today, your success vs. failure ratio, and your overall confidence. We need to rewire the memories you have formed and stored so that you can change your beliefs about failures into successes. Every unresolved negative emotion stays in your brain.

Where does the constant brain chatter come from? You're trying to sleep and your brain is going. Do you relive a past situation or conversation over and over again beating yourself up? Do you worry yourself into a frenzy over what you anticipate *might* happen? What is the cause? Fear. All the "what if" stories in your head, all the chaos when you want to sleep is created by fear. Your brain is just trying to make you feel safe and avoid pain, but it sure feels lousy.

There are several techniques available to you if you want to pursue the clearing of unresolved negative emotions. Of course there is traditional counseling, but that can take years. It is an effective technique, but no one technique is for everyone.

One technique is called NET, or the Neuro Emotional Technique. From their web site, "NET is a mind-body technique that uses a methodology of finding and removing neurological imbalances related to the physiology of unresolved stress. NET is a tool that can help improve many behavioral and physical conditions." The technique uses kinesiology, or muscle testing, to locate an imbalance in the body. We experience emotions every day, but when we fail to let go, we may find that we develop phobias, unexplained aversions, self-sabotaging behaviors, and/ or destructive beliefs. NET is helpful in getting unstuck from emotional patterns.

Your emotional reality can be different from your historical reality, or what really happened. Your perception of an event emotionally can affect your physical health. I bet you thought your emotions live in your brain. Sayings such as "a lump in your throat" or a feeling of butterflies in your stomach, demonstrate that emotions happen in other parts of the body too. I have included their web site in the resources section at the back of this book so you can learn more or find a practitioner.

EFT, the Emotional Freedom Technique, is also known as The Tapping Solution. According to their web site, "EFT is a powerful self-help method based on research showing that emotional trauma greatly contributes to disease. Clinical trials have shown that EFT is able to rapidly reduce the emotional impact of memories and incidents that trigger emotional distress. Once the distress is reduced or removed, the body can often rebalance itself, and accelerate healing." Please check the resources section for their web site address.

Reiki is a spiritual, Japanese technique for stress reduction and relaxation that also promotes healing. It involves the laying on of hands to move energy in the body. Some practitioners do not touch the body directly, but put their hands very close by.

If you are suffering from physical pain that no one has been able to diagnose or help you with, please seek one of these techniques to help you. If you suffered a traumatic loss or childhood, feel stuck, or can't stop your brain from its constant chatter, try one of these techniques. You will never know how physically and emotionally healthy you can feel unless you try.

Interestingly, if you'd like to know if you are more right brained or left brained there is a simple test. First, put your thumbs and forefingers together to create a triangle shape. Focus on a small object with your left eye and keep your right eye closed. Then, keeping your hands in the same place, close the left eye and look with your right. Whichever eye keeps the object in focus in the triangle shape is your dominant eye. Which foot would you kick a ball with? Which hand do you write with? Which ear do you put the phone up to when you need to listen carefully? (For example-someone is giving you directions.) Your dominant side is the one used most in those four scenarios. Cool, huh?

EXERCISE:

This is very interesting: by practicing a few rounds of alternate nostril breathing (called pranayama) daily, you can restore balance to your brain. Yogis also use this technique for better sleeping, calming the emotions, boosting one's thinking, and calming the nervous system. Did you know that you favor one nostril or the other almost all of the time?

The left nostril is associated with calming and the right for energy. Breathing in through the right nostril accesses the thinking or left side of your brain. Breathing though the left nostril accesses the right or feeling side of your brain.

This is how to do alternate nostril breathing:

1. Use your left thumb to close off your left nostril.
2. Inhale slowly and deeply through the right nostril.
3. Hold for a second or two.
4. Now close the right nostril with your right thumb.
5. Exhale through left nostril slowly and completely.
6. Now inhale through the left nostril.
7. Hold for a second or two.
8. Close off the left nostril and exhale through the right.

That is one round of alternate nostril breathing. Try to do two rounds and gradually increase the amount of rounds. Sit quietly for a few moments when you finish to enjoy the sensation.

SUCCESS ACRONYM

I decided to create an acronym for the word success for a few reasons. First of all, I thought it would break all of your reading into smaller chunks. That makes it easier to stop at a certain point to think over what you have read, or try putting one of the exercises into practice.

Sometimes you just run out of time to read, and I thought the acronym would make it easier for you to pick up where you left off, or to turn back a few pages to refresh what you have already read.

Also, our memories can only hold so much before we find ourselves on overload. Breaking the book into nice sized chunks will help you retain more and bridge from one section to the next. We are inundated with information from all sides all day long. How nice to sit down, (no TV, no cell phone or iPad) and relax with a new book for your self-improvement.

I believe the major aspects of success are building your stamina so you can face challenges and obstacles, and change your way of thinking about success and failure. Everything that happens to us, everything, can and should be used as a learning experience. Confidence and knowing how to gracefully accept a compliment are very important in success. Your emotional experiences can be viewed as baggage, or as the events that shaped who you are. Have you learned from them? Your experience on the planet depends on your self-worth and self-acceptance. Once you have accepted yourself and value yourself, you will have more to give others, and it will come back to you tenfold.

S tamina
U sed as a learning experience
C onfidence and compliments
C hange your core beliefs
E motional Experiences
S elf-worth
S elf-acceptance

CHAPTER ONE

STAMINA

*"Most of the important things in the world have been accomplished by people
who have kept on trying when there seemed to be no hope at all."*
~Dale Carnegie

As any Olympic athlete will tell you, stamina and endurance are a major part of winning. You get stamina through hard work and practice, by training and through experience. But how do you stay motivated for success day after day when you have felt like a failure?

The physical stamina from those Olympic athletes comes from the food they eat, the rest/sleep they allow themselves, and staying focused with their eye on the prize. All of us have to be in balance of body, mind, and spirit. Your physical well-being and health are important, but so is meeting your spiritual and emotional needs.

You can build up your success stamina in a few ways. First of all, think positive. I know. Sounds too simple, but it works. Changing your thoughts, changes your life. When you think positive, you feel good, and self-confidence builds until it is practically pouring out of you. People like to be with positive thinkers because their energy is high and contagious. You have trillions of cells in your body and they react to everything that your mind says. Negative thoughts and feelings can actually inhibit your immune system. Dr. Bruce Lipton says, "The moment you change your perception, is the moment you rewrite the chemistry of your body."

EXERCISE

Here is something you can try, right now. I love to write myself positive notes and thoughts on index cards. I bought myself a set of fine tipped Sharpie markers in a rainbow of colors. I write my positive thought on the center of the index card and then meditate on it as I draw with my markers all around the edges. I like to make swirls and shapes, sometimes small vines with flowers and leaves. But as I draw I feel more and more connected to the words I wrote. Then I place them all over my house. I have some by my front door, on my bookcase, on the fridge, near my calendar, on my nightstand, and I even carry some in my wallet. I have also been known to put them in the car. If you don't feel particularly artsy or maybe you don't like to draw at all, cut out pictures from magazines or download from the Internet. As long as there is meaning for you, those words will have you meditating on them and thinking about them in all situations of life. I keep the ones I'm not currently using in a basket. Sometimes I look through and reuse an old favorite too. You will feel your spirit lifting when you do this.

My favorite is, "Everything will be revealed to me in the perfect time space sequence."

You can also plan for setbacks. A setback is different than a failure, because your mind doesn't perceive it as permanent. It is temporary, minor and it does happen in life. What you do, how you react to a setback is what really matters. There is a difference between responding and reacting to all the blips on life's road. The basic difference is whether or not the situation gets better or is made worse.

Anxiety and anger are feelings associated with reacting. Often we beat ourselves up emotionally, and sometimes even physically, over what we perceive as our failures. Depending on your past experiences with failure, anxiety may be what you feel first, followed by anger. Or it could certainly be the other way around.

When presented with a situation in which you perceive a possibility of failing, anxiety may arise within you. These feelings of anxiousness can certainly lead right to what you so want to avoid. As we get more anxious and nervous, it is more difficult to think straight, to find the words we are searching for to express ourselves. Afterwards, we are angry at ourselves for not doing or saying what we had prepared. That subconscious mind we talked about before is smarter than our conscious mind. The Law of Attraction is simply: you get more of what you think about most of the time. Our subconscious mind is what makes that law work or not. And the subconscious learns by repetition, rehearsing the same thoughts over and over again.

Sometimes the anger comes first. You get angry with yourself for repeating the same scenario. You want to change and yet, somewhere deep inside, you are prevented from reacting the same way as you previously did.

How frustrating! Frustration can easily be played out through anger and we can turn it on ourselves through negative self-talk or even self-medicating in a variety of ways such as abusing alcohol and/or drugs, gambling, or even over-eating. Everyone has to eat, but controlling your food intake is essential to feeling healthy.

I was absolutely captivated by a reality TV show on the Style Network that was on a few years ago about a woman named Ruby Gettinger who brought her personal weight loss journey into the homes of millions of fans each week. Her top weight was 700 pounds and the show's producers sent in nutritionists and personal trainers to help Ruby hit a goal weight of 250 pounds. During the airing of the show, several emotional issues came to light, that never really seemed to be resolved. Ruby "forgot" several years of her childhood. She has no memory of schools she attended, homes she lived in, nothing. It is like that part of her memory was erased. The show ended suddenly and left all us fans wondering what happened. It seems Ruby was not having the success in her weight loss that was expected by the producers. She also managed to sabotage herself at every turn, even going so far as to disguise herself going through a McDonald's drive-thru. She personally detailed in an interview how she would starve herself then binge, or shift her weight during a weigh-in showing a loss when there was none.

Ruby, wherever you are, I wish you well. I have a feeling that whatever happened to you in the time period you cannot remember was and continues to be too painful for you to deal with. Eating has been the way you have learned to self-medicate, but it doesn't really make you feel better, does it? Please don't give up! I hope you find someone who can help you deal with the pain from your past, so you can begin to live a healthy future.

I know for me in my earlier years, I was filled with anger. It could erupt at any time and surprise me as well as the unsuspecting recipient. I wondered where it came from. I wondered why it was so intense. Afterward, I was left drained and feeling anxious about what others were thinking about me. It was like I had a different personality when angry.

When you respond, you can look at what is happening, and understand what you are feeling, and reflect on it. The point is that you can stop and think, and hopefully withhold judgment. When you respond, rather than react, you have a sense of control because you can see options and choices. A reaction is impulsive, you an immediate behavioral response. Reactions are based strictly on emotions without an opportunity to think and use your intellect.

For your personal growth, understanding this difference is immense. Knowing you have options is empowering for anyone. Knowing you may have more control over circumstances than you thought is even better.

Responding, rather than reacting, will get you closer to success in all areas of your life. It demonstrates an ability to control your emotions, make well thought out decisions, and removes a victim mentality.

EXERCISE:

So, to build your stamina, try keeping a gratitude journal and developing a grateful attitude in everyday life. Every day, driving to work, speaking with co-workers or family members, noticing a rainbow in the sky, anything and everything can be a source of that most wonderful feeling of being grateful. Try to bring all of your senses to a new height: see the colors of the world, smell the delicious aromas of a home cooked meal, or literally stop and smell the roses. Feel the textures of things around you: the smoothness of the granite countertop, the softness of your pet's fur. Listen to the sound of a small plane flying overhead, wonder where those people are going. Daydream. Feel. Think. Be.

Some people like to write in their journal in the morning, others in the evening. I love to write so my journal is with me all the time and I add to it as I go through the day. If you are in a relationship, share your gratefulness with your partner. Practice expressing gratitude for each other too. All of us want to feel loved and appreciated for the little things too.

I had a client I will call Mary. When we first began to work together, Mary was just about to turn 40 yet had been unable to hold a steady job for any amount of time. Every new job was her "dream job", it was a "perfect fit", but not for long. Within the first few weeks, she would go to work full of enthusiastic ideas. They would be bursting out of her. She had ways to make everything better from boosting employee morale to changing major corporate policy. Well, needless to say, this didn't go over very well from the new kid on the block. Soon Mary's resume was 14 pages long! Not a promising sign to a prospective employer.

At first Mary didn't understand why her new bosses were not as enthusiastic about her ideas as she was, so she would leave and start all over again with a new employer. Mary went from job to job, employer to employer feeling that she was being singled out and victimized by each and every one of them. It was too difficult for her to see that she could not just walk in as the new kid on the block, tell everyone what they were doing wrong, and that she was now here to deliver them from all their business problems because she, and she alone, had figured out what was wrong and how to make it right. No one appreciated her attitude of superiority, when that was not her intention at all. What a lack of communication!

This continued for almost 15 years before Mary was finally able to see the pattern that had developed. After all, in every situation, there was one and only one common factor-Mary! She had not held any one job for more than a year and a half and left every employer feeling unappreciated for her creative ideas.

Once we had established that Mary could see the pattern and was absolutely determined to make changes in her life, I asked her to start from an attitude of gratitude. Feeling thankful, for even the smallest things in life, helps to make us feel happier and more positive. Mary had trouble that first time coming up with five things she felt grateful for, but with time, she was filling notebooks. Then I asked Mary to begin a list of all her strengths in every aspect of her life. She is a good organizer. She is a people person. Her brain is always cooking up new and exciting ideas because she is so creative. She was able to fill a whole sheet of paper-front and back.

The next step was to get very specific and write down her absolute ideal dream job. I asked her to describe it in such detail that it became real to her. I wanted her to see the layout, the furniture, smell the office supplies, envision who was around her, what she was wearing head to toe. This was not a quickie exercise, but one that built over several sessions of us working together. It is not easy to look at yourself with a critical yet loving eye to create a better tomorrow for yourself.

Mary soon realized that she was an idea person. She loves ideas. Her brain doesn't stop. Everything she looks at just turns into a million ideas in her head. But…she is not a person of action. Having the ideas is exciting, but the stamina for follow through was lacking. She didn't have the technical expertise to make her dreams a reality. So, Mary set out to find the right someone who could take an idea and make it happen. She formed a business in which her constant flow of ideas works well. Her two partners are people of action with the technical ability to turn her ideas into marketable items. Their business is off to a great start and she loves the freedom of being able to unleash her creativity.

Previously, Mary did not have the stamina she needed to create her pathway to success in any job because she walked in and was ready to be CEO before she had learned the ins and outs of the particular business. She didn't start with an attitude of joining a team.

Another client of mine, Tim, had just finished his junior year at a local university. He was confused. Every time he was sure he knew what he wanted to study, he would take a class or two, hit a wall, and change his major. He could not handle any criticism or any grade less than an A. He was such a perfectionist, that he didn't give himself a chance to really learn and experience a particular course of study. By the time we met, he was thinking of quitting school, and working in his uncle's business until he could come up with a better idea.

Tim needed to build some stamina, to give his studies more of a chance before quitting and walking away. Perfectionists live in fear, so they can never enjoy their success. They often procrastinate to put off being judged. Tim could not understand his need for being perfect. He said it wasn't from pressure at home, but he felt driven to be the best. If he felt he could not achieve that, he would stay in his dorm room and withdraw from friends and family.

So we started by discussing possible situations that could take place in which Tim would still be considered a success, even if not perfect. At first, he was very nervous. He sat wringing his hands, he broke out in a sweat, and his breathing quickened. And this was just an imagination game. Once Tim was able to imagine the absolute worst case scenario and realize it wasn't as bad as he'd thought, we were able to build up some stamina for him to go out into the real world and be less than perfect, just like the rest of us.

Tim had a problem dealing with any of his negative emotions, so he held himself to a standard that no one could possibly achieve. When he let himself down by being less than perfect, he caused himself untold emotional suffering. Tim's life changed over time as he accepted imperfection and learned how to deal with his negative emotions. He graduated from the university and had several job offers to choose from the last time we met.

CHAPTER TWO

USED AS A LEARNING EXPERIENCE

*"There is only one thing more painful than learning from
experience, and that is not learning from experience."*
~Laurence J. Peter

Success takes planning and stamina, and more than a little patience. Bill Gates dropped out of Harvard and started a business that failed. Today we know him as the successful creator of the global empire Microsoft. Walt Disney was once fired for having a lack of imagination. He also had a bankruptcy and several other business failures. Today those Disney theme parks earn billions each year. Can you believe twenty seven different publishers rejected Dr. Seuss's first book!

Babe Ruth held more than his most famous record of most home runs. He held the record for most strike outs too. With great success comes risk. Are you willing to take a risk on a new relationship? Go for that promotion at work? Dan Wells, Latter-Day Saint author said, "Until you've given yourself permission to fail, you will never succeed."

So you have two choices. You can fail to learn or learn by failing. The failure mindset uses failure as an excuse, while the person with a positive mindset views each try as getting them closer to their desired outcome.

Patterns form. Failures happen. People come and go in your life. You move. You get a job. Before you know it, failure becomes part of your daily mental map, and you are in a trap. How easy it is to blame all of your shortcomings on other people, places or situations. Having an excuse prevents you from moving forward and making positive changes in your life. The worst part of it all is that even though it seems to you be OK to place blame, it is perceived by others as the excuse it actually is.

Becoming a victim of circumstances is a choice. That may feel harsh at this point, but as you keep reading, you will realize how much of your victimization is something you have nurtured and developed, rather than learning from and letting go.

Thomas Edison did poorly in school and his teacher thought him incapable of being able to learn. His mother pulled him out and home schooled him. Although he had little formal education, (about three months) he was mechanically inclined. He eventually held 1, 093 U.S. Patents in his name. He is most well-known for inventing the light bulb, phonograph, and motion picture camera, however, from the rejection of his very first invention, Edison did not give up. He literally went through over 10,000 prototypes of the light bulb before he reached success. He considered every prototype an elimination of a way that would not work, rather than as a failure. Where would he be today if he had not used each attempt as a learning experience?

"Failure is not the opposite of success,
It is an integral part of it."
~Arianna Huffington

My client Roma comes to my mind when I think of learning experiences. She was married for thirty-three years, had three children, an active social and church life and from the outside looking in everything seemed wonderful. She thought so too. Until one day, she came home to find her husband sitting on the edge of the bed and he told her he didn't love her and that he never had! Well, she was demolished, crushed, and destroyed.

"Convert difficulties into opportunities,
for difficulties are divine surgeries to make you better."
~Author Unknown

When we met, she was in a deep depression. She didn't leave the house for almost two weeks, and cried until she really feared she would never stop. Everything froze in time for her from that moment. She was unable to work, care for her children, or even function on the most basic level. She was filled with grief, shame and embarrassment. Getting out of bed became a major task, and so her bedroom became the place where we first began working together.

First of all, Roma's grief was real and certainly justified. To get her to a level of acceptance of her current situation, I asked her to write. I asked to write about her relationship from the beginning to that day. I asked her to write how she felt and feels. I asked her to pour it all out of her insides onto paper. When we next met, she had pages and pages. We discussed how she felt after writing it all down, and I could see on her face that she had purged. I asked her to create a ceremony for cleansing once and for all. She drove to the beach one evening, set up her chair, and read the pages one last time. She then burned them! Yes, she burned them and then she was ready to begin a new chapter in her life.

Roma needed to get moving so we started with walking. Up the block, then around the block, then 5 mile walks. As she walked, rather than music, she would recite the alphabet from A-Z thinking of every positive word she could think of. For example: A=abundance, B=beautiful, C=cheerful, D=delighted, etc… This really helped her to change her thinking and begin to feel much better.

Roma began to get out of the house once again and to socialize with close family and friends. We discussed how she could ask for the kind of support she needed emotionally. We also changed her diet. I had her add an oil blend of omega 3-6-9 and more fruits and vegetables. Soon she was able to comfort her children who were filled with anger and resentment toward their father. Roma developed some affirmations for herself to keep her thinking positively. She was also surprised to find that she loved yoga. She told me, "I thought yoga was about twisting my body into impossible pretzel shapes. I had no idea how empowered I could feel." This was all a process, but she was a new person.

"A bend in the road is not the end of the road…
unless you fail to make the turn."
~Author Unknown

Sometimes it is hard to notice a pattern in your life. The people involved, the events may be different, but the underlying pattern is still there. Even if someone points it out for us, we still may not be able to see it-kind of like the saying "can't see the forest for the trees." Obviously, if you can't see the pattern, you can't make the changes to grow; you can't turn those experiences into a lesson learned.

Tom Bodett says, "The difference between school and life? In school, you're taught a lesson, then given a test. In life, you're given a test that teaches you a lesson."

How can you learn to recognize the patterns? Awareness. You need to become more aware and more in touch with whom you really are. As you develop your self-awareness, you will notice certain aspects of your personality that normally would have been ignored. With practice, you will be able to make better choices in the way you think opening up possibilities for change.

Life is changing all the time all around us. You change too. You are not who you were as a toddler or elementary school student. However, sometimes your mind tries to stay the same. You don't question it, you might not even be aware of it, but your thoughts have not kept up with the other changes. Your mind is able to keep up a constant chattering that distracts you and also in many ways controls you. Eckert Tolle has written several books about this.

Have you ever felt like you are on a roller coaster of emotions? Too much drama in your life? Overwhelmed by shame or guilt? You can actually become addicted to those emotions and create more of what you *don't* want. Remember, from <u>The Secret:</u> where you put your attention, what you focus on is what gets manifested in your life.

People who have developed their self-awareness speak openly and honestly, are able to view a perceived mistake as a learning opportunity, and show the world a confident, happy individual.

"When you lose, don't lose the lesson."
~Unknown

When you make a mistake, what happens? What goes on inside your head? Do you beat yourself up? Call yourself names? Wish you could hit rewind and start all over again now that you know the outcome? You are just causing your own suffering. How much better for you, and all those close to you, if you could see that same mistake as a growth opportunity.

Remember, everything changes. Nothing in this world is stagnant because every single thing is vibrating energy. Practice taking responsibility for all you say and do. My own daughter struggled with the two words, "I'm sorry" for her whole childhood. Take ownership. Know everyone can make a mistake, learn from it, and move on. If you prefer, don't use the word "failure" or "mistake". Think of words like "obstacle", "challenge", or even "roadblock". To me they sound more positive. Be open to changing, looking at the same old situation with a new perspective. If you look for the lesson, you will see it.

There are two mistakes one can make along the road to
truth-not going all the way, and not starting."
~Buddha

I think the most important thing to remember about success here is that failure is not final. If you do not take a risk, you will never know how wonderful the outcome could be. If you do not try, you cannot fail, but you also cannot make any progress in your relationships, employment, or spiritual areas of your life. Are you content with things the way they are?

How you feel about making a mistake was probably learned in your early childhood. Perhaps a parent, grandparent, teacher or some other authority figure ridiculed you. Maybe your classmates laughed at you. I had an awful experience with peer pressure when I had just started junior high school. A Slam Book was circulated through the school. I was a lowly seventh grader, and didn't even know what a Slam Book was. (By the way it is a notebook with people's names at the top of all the pages. On the front page everyone picks a number, signs in, and then uses that number throughout the book to write what they think of the person whose name appears at the top of the page.)

My friends and I were in the bathroom, when in walked the cool eighth graders. The leader of the pack kicked my books across the floor, and told me to meet her after school where she was going to kick my butt for what I wrote about her and her friends in the book. I turned around and my friends were gone. I was terrified all day. I snuck over to a friend's house to avoid her and called my mom to pick me up. My Mom turned to me and asked, "So, what are you going to do tomorrow? And the next day? The day after that?"

I knew I had never written a word in that book, but how was I going to convince her of that? I didn't know her. She didn't know me. Who had written those words in my name? I couldn't eat. I couldn't sleep. I was completely enveloped in dread. No previous experiences with being unjustly accused or bullied could have prepared me for what I was about to face. Somehow, from somewhere deep within myself, I found the guts to make the decision to show up and face that group of girls at the end of the next school day.

I don't remember anything about the day itself. The hours passed, I attended classes, and then the moment of truth arrived, my personal moment of facing my fear. My school was quite old, and I pushed through the heavy wooden door and stepped outside under the white columned portico, my heart beating through my chest. The girl and her friends stepped up to me, and surrounded me. I remember blinking and swallowing hard but nothing else.

Again, the leader of the group accused me and again I denied it. I told her I didn't even know what a Slam Book was and that I still hadn't even seen the one she was referring to. Suddenly the doors burst open and the girl who stood there was the toughest girl in the school, in the whole neighborhood probably. I knew her name. She had asked me for help in class a few times and I tutored her once or twice during lunch before a test. I remember her playfully punching my arm and thanking me for helping her earn a "C" on a test in Social Studies.

She broke through the circle of girls, actually I think they parted for her to pass through, and she threw an arm around my shoulder. She told them I was a good kid and her friend. She told them if they messed with me, they messed with her. And just like that it was all over. They turned and left, and so did she. She walked away and there I stood, all alone, feeling lucky!

That experience of fear stayed with me for years, but so did that feeling of standing up for myself. It influenced where I would go and who I would be with. I felt very uncomfortable at parties with large groups of people. I spent many years feeling judged by others every time I opened my mouth. But I did learn to champion for justice and what I really believed to be right. I still trembled. I still shook with fear. I still couldn't eat or sleep. I chose carefully, but there were several times I really stood up ready to take a fall if necessary.

Through counseling, emotional balancing with NET (Neuro Emotional Technique), EFT(Emotional Freedom Technique, also known as the Tapping Solution) and Reiki, I have learned from my emotional experiences and am happier for it. I can now face an unstable situation feeling strong and capable, without that crippling fear. Before, I was missing out on living my life, because I was afraid. I was either reliving the past, or worriedly anticipating the future. I worked hard on building my feelings of being safe and secure. It took time, but now I live my life with joy and gratitude. Not all the time, my life isn't perfect, but I grab every bit of love and excitement I can.

There are definite things you can do for your brain. It will thank you. You have heard them all before. Quit smoking. Get a good night's sleep. Follow a diet incorporating lots of veggies and some fruit and eliminate sugar. Limit your hours of TV. Exercise to get your endorphins pumping. Set yourself free from alcohol and drugs. When I talk with my clients about alcohol, 99% of them think it is normal and healthy to have a drink or two every day to "unwind" and "relax". "Alcohol is not the answer. It just makes you forget the question." Drugs, whether recreational or prescription, cause a change in brain chemistry.

The brain is something we all take for granted but it requires care. It is the most important organ in your body. You use it for everything from deciding what to eat or what to wear, to what makes you laugh or cry (the emotional brain), your core beliefs about yourself (also the emotional brain) and the very thoughts you think.

EXERCISE:

Think back to your earliest memories of feeling like a failure. Draw a rough sketch of where you were, who was with you, and the circumstances. Then just add labels to your sketch. Then walk away for a few days and when you return revisit this sketch with new eyes. Now this is the past and you are an adult with an adult way of looking at things. Write a letter to your younger hurt self and reassure yourself that everything is going to be alright, because it already is.

CHAPTER THREE

CONFIDENCE AND COMPLIMENTS

*"Smile, for everyone lacks self-confidence and
more than any other one thing, a smile reassures them."*
~Andre Maurois

Don't you love to meet someone who just exudes confidence? You know you are in the right place with the right person at the right time. It is so comforting in these stressful times, to find someone who can and will actually help you. Self-confident people have traits we all admire. Confidence is attractive, while downplaying it is not. Many women in our society have been taught that it is immodest to be too outwardly confident. Not true!

A common pitfall in those who lack confidence, is to view it in others as conceit, mockery or even manipulation. One who is conceited has an exaggerated opinion while one who is confident has no uncertainties. It may seem a fine line, but it makes a difference. Conceited people are constantly trying to prove something. People are generally drawn to confidence because there is a certain amount of humbleness there. You feel welcomed, you feel like you are an equal, and people just relax around those feelings. If you feel you are being mocked, it is as if the whole world stops spinning momentarily and all eyes and ears are on you! You feel the red flush of shame creep up your neck to your face and you cringe inside! No one wants to be the butt of a joke! Manipulation comes across at first as charm, a flashy white smile, a squeeze of your hand and you are putty. But then the thought comes in, "Oh he's just saying that so I will do what he wants."

When someone gives you praise or a compliment, do you squirm? Deflecting praise is based in fear. We wouldn't want someone to get the wrong idea about us. To gain confidence, you need to learn to love and accept yourself. You've heard it said a million times that no one is perfect, but do you hold yourself to a higher level anyway? Of course, you will be disappointed. Self-confident, self-loving people exude openness and usually have a genuine smile and look you right in the eye with warmth and understanding. Those traits can be practiced. With each success, you will want to do more and more. I recommend that you accept the praise or compliment. Trust that no one is out to get you and that it is genuine. Instead of deflecting the compliment, simply say "Thank you." That's it.

The failure mindset interprets repeated failures as signals to stop trying, give up. Successful people try and when it works they continue to use the same technique over and over building upon their success. There are two ways you can approach this. We need to be realistic about the situation we find ourselves in. The saying goes that "it takes two to tango", so what is your role in repeating failures? We can use those failures to make ourselves sick and unhappy or to make ourselves strong.

One way is to try and hope. The second way, which may offer you more success, is to do. That's it. Do it. Go out and do something new and different. The feeling is empowering. I believe each and every one of us was put on this earth to live out our purpose and do it fearlessly.

It is said that to create a habit something needs to be repeated 21 times! That's a lot! 21 times! Can you believe that you have developed a pattern of perceiving yourself or your life as a failure this many times? Your thoughts are powerful. They create the life you are living at this moment. All your previous thoughts have produced the feelings, emotions, thoughts, and imaginings of the present moment. Are you happy? Self-confident people inspire confidence in others. Self-confidence can be learned if you feel this is something blocking your feeling of success.

It is essential, I repeat essential, that you learn how to take compliments graciously. As you exude more confidence in yourself, people will look up to you, and you will receive more compliments. In childhood we are taught to be modest, so we may deflect a compliment. Take it in. Bask in the feeling. Be appreciative. A successful, confident person knows their self-worth and appreciates acknowledgment. Do not rebuff or redirect a compliment. It is simple, merely smile and say, "Thank you." As you feel more comfortable accepting compliments you can expand your response, but keeping things simple always works.

Lighten up. Some people take a compliment the wrong way. Their own lack of confidence causes them to look for sarcasm and falseness. You may need to practice in the mirror, but be proud. Use positive body language by making direct eye contact. Be patient with yourself if this is new to you. You might want to have a handy reply ready to pull out if you feel uncomfortable or embarrassed when you receive a compliment.

EXERCISE:

One way to build your confidence so you can accept a compliment is to recognize your own talents and best qualities. You will need a notebook for this exercise. Get comfortable. Relax. Start a timer for five minutes and open your notebook. Begin to list all of the things about yourself that you admire. They can be physical characteristics, personality traits, past achievements, whatever. Write for five minutes. Do not stop until that timer goes off. Some people get off to a slow start and then are still writing when the timer sounds. Do this every few months and see how your confidence grows.

There is a saying "fake it 'til you make it." This goes for confidence building. If you have mastered the art of blending in and being mostly invisible, start by changing one aspect of your clothing, hair, shoes, or even eyeglasses. Start to wear a smile every day, wherever you are. I once walked into work on a Monday morning and a colleague said to me, "You are always smiling. It makes everyone around you feel happier." Anyone can wear a smile. They're free. You start to convince yourself by faking it until you really start to feel it. Also, practice making eye contact when you speak with others. If you feel uncomfortable, practice in front of a mirror or with a close friend or family member. It touches a person's heart to look into your eyes. There is another saying about the eyes being the window to one's soul. It's true.

Pursue your passion! Photography? Painting? Travel? Writing? Perhaps starting up your own business? If it comes from the heart and stirs your passion, it will do the same for others you meet. People are animated when they talk about what they love. Once you start to talk about what you love, others will become captivated. What a great confidence booster and opportunity to receive compliments.

Mandy completely lacked self-confidence. She was extremely shy, tried to hide, and rarely smiled. She lived alone and kept her world very small so she could avoid as much public exposure as possible. In her late twenties, she looked at least 20 years older. She had no siblings, her parents had both passed on, and other than her nine to five job, she was all alone in the world.

After the attacks on the World Trade Center in 2001, she begged her boss to be able to work from home. She would order groceries by phone and have them delivered. A few years later, she had not even stepped into the hallway of her building to get her mail. A neighbor was kind enough to slide it under her door. Everything and everyone created mind numbing fear in Mandy. She was a shell of the person she once was.

I met Mandy through her neighbor. We had been serving on a committee together and met at her home. She told me the story of her recluse neighbor over a cup of coffee and I was astounded. One day, around 10:30 in the morning, Mandy heard a terrible thud from the apartment upstairs. She knew an elderly woman who used a walker lived there alone. Her son would come to visit on the weekends, but this was a Tuesday morning. Mandy began to pace. What could she do? The anxiety caused her to begin to cry and wring her hands helplessly. It was out of the question for her to leave the apartment to go upstairs and check on the woman. She paced. She fretted. She cried.

About an hour later, she heard soft cries like from a baby. Soft pitiful little sobs. It sounded like a combination of crying and moaning. Finally, her compassion for another human being overpowered her own fears to the point that she went up the stairs. She had no thoughts for herself at that moment. The door was slightly ajar, and there on the floor was not the elderly lady she expected but a young man, maybe 35 years old. He was out cold on the floor. But the cries that stirred the compassion in Mandy's heart were from a little kitten curled up next to the man.

Very long story, shortened, the young man was a severe epileptic and had suffered a seizure. Mandy called an ambulance; they fell in love and married. She continued to work from home, but with love and patience on his part, was soon able to venture out into the community. Her ability to love and trust changed her whole life.

> *"We gain strength, and courage and confidence by each experience*
> *in which we really stop to look fear in the face…*
> *we must do that which we think we cannot."*
> *~Eleanor Roosevelt*

How would you rate your confidence level right now? Hopefully you are somewhere between fair and heading toward invincible. Did you know the number 1 fear in the world is the fear of public speaking? Remember when you were a kid and Mom told you not to talk to strangers? That idea is deeply embedded in your psyche from childhood. As you grew older, you were given permission to do things such as ride your bike off the block, or drive a car, or even cross the street by yourself. You were never given permission to talk to strangers. Maybe it is time to change that fear. As of this moment, you are hereby granted permission to talk to strangers.

If the thought of talking in front of a group of people still scares the daylights out of you, even with your newly acquired permission, perhaps you want to look into Toastmasters International. This is an international organization devoted to helping people improve their public speaking and listening skills through positive reinforcement in their weekly meetings. This organization is a world leader in communication and leadership development. Their membership, as of today, is 292,000 strong. These members improve their speaking and leadership skills by attending one of the 13,500 clubs in 116 countries that make up their global network of meeting locations.

Part of your definition of success must include climbing the ladder in your workplace, community, or other organization. Leadership skills and better communication of both speaking and listening are essential to your success. Again, let the mirror be your friend. Practice speaking, making eye contact, and smiling. Remember a smile is the same in every language, culture and region of the world.

"Take advantage of every opportunity to practice your communication skills so that when important occasions arise, you will have the gift, the style, the sharpness, the clarity, and the emotions to affect people."
~Jim Rohn

Confidence in you is the key to self-acceptance and self-worth. These will be discussed further in chapters six and seven. Just know that how you perceive yourself is communicated to others whether you are aware of it or not. People have a sense of what feels genuine and what is forced. People recognize when you value yourself and your time and your gifts. It is sort of like the age old question: what came first the chicken or the egg? Well what came first: the things that have happened in your life to diminish your confidence and how you feel about yourself and carry yourself OR how you have been thinking about yourself and the way you carry yourself? Food for thought, isn't it?

You will hear me say many times throughout this book that what you put your focus on is what you will attract into your life. If you think about what you don't have, such as confidence, you will have more *lack* of confidence. It is important to build yourself up by focusing on your gifts. What you may be taking for granted because it comes easily and naturally to you, may be harder than Chinese algebra to someone else. We all have gifts. Figure out yours and your confidence will zoom!

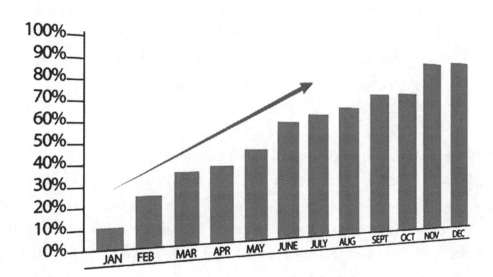

CHAPTER FOUR

CHANGE YOUR CORE BELIEFS

*"The world we see that seems so insane is the result of a belief system
that is not working. To perceive the world differently, we must be
willing to change our belief system, let the past slip away, expand
our sense of now, and dissolve the fear in our minds."*
~William James

Your core beliefs are the foundation upon which you react or respond in a particular situation. By way of the Law of Attraction, your core beliefs act like energy magnets drawing to you what you focus upon. Deep core beliefs start in early childhood. They are so subtle you are not aware they exist, but they form so early in your life, that they become embedded deep inside you. You act and behave in a certain way that supports or suppresses your success and personal power. The way you do not think about breathing or making your heart beat, your core beliefs are like a knee-jerk response. Core beliefs are those things you know and trust to be your truth.

Core beliefs were meant to be temporary, until you were mature enough to take charge of your own life. We learn from our families what the definition of success is from the time we are very young. It is modeled for us by our parents and extended family in many ways. We may learn a particular set point for success that becomes embedded in us as a deep core belief that we accept and never question. No matter how young you were when your core belief developed, you still believe it.

This is not to say that your core beliefs are wrong, bad, or even dysfunctional. When you were a child you had a limited ability to discern conclusions from whatever your particular experiences were. Your perceptions from that time were just right. Are they still today? If it were possible that you could go back and watch the circumstances under which you formed your core beliefs with the views of your adult self, you would understand the why's and how's of them. There is an emotional reaction when an event triggers a core belief that you perceive as "truth". That sets off a chain reaction of that voice in your head telling you, "You can't do it!"

The good news is that core beliefs are not rigid. You can change them. When you come up against an obstacle, you may want to take time to reflect what you are feeling. Your beliefs are simply thoughts you repeatedly think. Like a habit, it can be changed but will need some work.

First of all, you need to become more aware of your thoughts. Every time you think a negative thought, express an unhappiness in your mind, you are attracting more of the same. My friend Val likes to use the expression, "I get to..." to turn a negative into a positive. Rather than dwelling on what you dislike about your job, you change your thoughts to, "I get to go to work. I get to appreciate the job I have now." Try to be aware of your thoughts, you might be amazed.

Also, remember that your neocortex, or rational brain, is doing many jobs all at once. It is thinking, deciding, problem solving at the same time it is taking in all kinds of information from the outside world. Your core beliefs are at work keeping you safe and protected. Beliefs inherited from your family, may have worked in the past, but you need to question them now. Do they serve me well? Are they holding me back from the success I desire? You can rewrite your story as you go along, but repeated successes will make it easier over time as your confidence builds.

Too bad we cannot go back in time to discover when and how our core beliefs were formed. Every family experiences problems and there is yet to be a perfect parent. Remember, you live what you believe. My parents struggled financially throughout most of my life. They even lost our family home and moved to several apartments until resettling down. Needless to say, I developed some core beliefs about money, or at least lack of money. New ways of thinking and/or new ideas for growth were not accepted or encouraged, because my parents were into keeping all of us safe and protected.

I took a job for several years that didn't pay me enough to cover all my bills each month! My self-esteem was crushed and I was indebted to my boss to extend me small loans continually. I finally realized he had pegged many of his employees into that situation so he could hold over our heads how good he had been to us. When I left that job, he was angry with me, but I felt free!

Core beliefs are not something that comes from the mind; rather they hold your mind. I was finally able to go out into the world with a fresh, new mindset. I expected to be successful and little by little it came to pass. I went back to school for a master's degree in education and my ability to earn a good salary increased tenfold. I was able to tutor privately and earn extra money, especially during the summer. Teachers are not notoriously well paid, but with my confidence growing, I was paid to spend a week training teachers at an elementary school in Belle Glade, Florida how to teach writing to their students. I have had many opportunities for success that I never would have anticipated before.

Your ability to attract what you want into your life is the strongest when it is also what you expect to happen. Alignment of those two parts is critical. Back to "The Secret" once again-you attract into your life what you focus upon. If you deeply believe that you can't do something, then it should not be a surprise when you actually can't. And vice versa too. You may have to let go of the limiting beliefs you assumed as a child that no longer serve you.

A friend of mine shared this story with me recently. When she was fifteen years old, and learning how to drive, her father sat next to her in the front passenger seat repeating over and over again, "Just stay in your lane. You're fine if you just stay in your lane." She never really gave it much thought until recently, more than forty years later, she realized she rarely if ever changes lanes when she is driving. Suddenly, she noticed a car in front of her driving very slowly and all the cars behind her pulling out, changing lanes, and traveling at the speed limit past her. It occurred to her that she could still hear her Dad's voice telling her, "Just stay in your lane. Just stay in your lane." And the good daughter that she is, she was still doing so.

This is a perfect example of how we can totally accept a core belief and not question it, even if it no longer serves us well. To me it seems her Dad was quite nervous as a passenger with a new driver and *he* felt safe if she just stayed in her lane. His fear was adopted by her as a driving principle to be strictly adhered to for the rest of her life. I am not sure what caught her attention that day and made her aware that she is safe to change lanes, but it happened. Awareness of who you are, what you believe, and a balance of body, mind, and spirit opens your life to limitless possibilities of good.

You can consciously use the Law of Attraction to create the life you want to live. You can let go of your own fears and those you have learned from others. You can change your life by changing the thoughts you think when you become aware of what they are. Trust yourself. Trust in yourself. It is all for your greatest good. Worry, anxiety, anticipation get you nowhere. Those emotions can even make you sick, which you will read more about in the next chapter. Negative feelings that you focus on, bring you more of the same.

Want to reinforce all of your fears and negative core beliefs? It's easy. Sit in front of the TV all day. Watch the 24 hour news stations, listen to politicians and commentators and you will be drowning in negativity within the first ten minutes.

I grew up in New York on Long Island. Later as an adult, I moved to Canarsie, Brooklyn. I have lived in other countries and other states, but to this day I am a New Yorker in my heart. I sound like one too. I was living in South Florida when the Twin Towers were destroyed. At first, I thought I was looking at coming attractions for a new movie. Once I realized this was no movie, I was glued to the TV. That September day I literally watched CNN continually for about 8 hours. Over and over again I saw the planes hit and the towers fall. Eric came and stood in front of the TV. I was bleary eyed. He said, "Enough. Turn the TV off. You are not doing yourself or any of the other suffering people any good." I turned the TV off that night, and have not sat and watched a newscast since.

How many of us grew up watching TV during dinner? Or our parents watched last thing before turning the TV off for the night. Wouldn't it just make sense that the last thing you watch will stay with you all night in your dreams? I wonder how people get restful sleep at night watching the 10:00 News?

It seems to me that TV is the ultimate in passivity. The shows, news, and especially the commercials are telling you what you like, what you want, and what you need. Do you stop to think if any of it is true for you? The advertisers are good, they are smooth, that is their job-to sell you. They want to persuade you to take your money and buy what they have convinced you that you need. You will be happy with this car. You will look successful wearing this designer. You will be healthy eating these foods.

Well, as you already know, you can't buy your happiness. Nope. It is not something that is outside of you waiting for you to turn the next corner and find it. If you are struggling with what you were taught in the past, you are limiting your personal power. My energy and power are too important to me to just give away. It takes consciousness and courage on your part to be able to recognize and choose to surrender outdated teachings (core beliefs) when they are interfering in your happiness today. Let me warn you that those core beliefs are comfortable. Unless you are willing to search, they will be hard to find. Like my friend who drove for forty years not changing lanes, it suddenly dawned on her one day, "Why not?" She knows herself to be a safe driver. She trusts herself behind the wheel. Yes, she can change lanes. It is OK.

Back at the beginning of this book, you read about how your conscious brain works. That part of your brain I referred to as the neo-cortex or mammalian brain, which controls your interactions with and understanding of the world. This includes using your five senses, problem solving and also keeping you safe by listening to the directions from your core beliefs.

When you notice a negative thought, let it go. Some people like to imagine putting it on a cloud or balloon and watching it drift away. Other people literally stop themselves and say, "Cancel. Cancel. Cancel." I like to imagine a white board and visualize myself erasing the negative thought. As you become more aware and play with some of these options, you will find what works best for you. Do not misunderstand me here. I am not saying negative thoughts are bad. Thoughts are things that are neither good nor bad. But certainly, I know I don't want to waste my energy by indulging in negative emotions. Remember, the thought comes before the emotion. What are you thinking? Will that thought help the Law of Attraction bring you what you want or more of what you don't want?

CHAPTER FIVE

EMOTIONAL EXPERIENCES

"It is the mind which creates the world around us,
and even though we stand side by side in the same meadow,
my eyes will never see what is beheld by yours,
my heart will never stir to the emotions with which yours is touched."
~George Gissing

All experiences are emotional. You store them in the limbic part of your brain. You form neural nets that hold those emotions for you to refer back to the next time that same emotion arises inside of you. Joy, love, ecstasy, vulnerability, loss, and pain; all of it goes into and stays stored in the emotional part of your brain.

Your parents are your first hypnotists. They form your core beliefs by what they do and say. They teach you to fear, to be careful, and to avoid. The intention is to keep you safe, but you learn fear. The belief in a label that someone attaches to your condition, childhood and innocence, keeps the condition in place, empowers it, and makes a seemingly solid reality. Remember your brain is involved in everything you do. The limbic system is your emotional brain. This is where bonding takes place and of course you trust your very first caregivers implicitly.

A feeling of loss, whether real or perceived, can be so overwhelming for a child. Children just do not perceive the world in the same way adults do, and they can take on responsibility for things that are not their own. The death of someone close to you, that you relied on, that you needed, can create a void that is easily filled in ways that can hurt or even destroy you, inside and out. Every child I have ever worked with who struggled with the divorce of his or her parents, actually thought that in some way it was their fault.

I have worked with young children for almost 30 years. I have seen children who come from loving, supportive parents who do not appreciate or reflect the morals and attitudes of the home. They have everything they could possibly want. The parents work hard, and lavishly pay for sports, clothing, toys, vacations, and whatever else their children desire. They want their children to have their wishes fulfilled.

In our culture, we spend money, buy things, and sometimes the kids don't seem to show an iota of appreciation. We are left feeling awful-used and unappreciated even though we work hard for our money to buy them nice things and take them the places they'd like to go. But from the nine year old point of view, what does he know about money? What does she know of financial pressures? If we tempt them to behave and reward them by buying things, what can we realistically expect? They will just want more. They will not develop the inner motivation needed to want to do a good job. They will become reliant upon extrinsic enticements.

I know an eight year old who told me, "If I can be good for the next week, my parents are going to buy me my own iPad." I replied, "Wow! What are you going to do with an iPad?" He answered, "Play with the app Photo Booth." I waited for more. There was nothing else forthcoming. Hmmmm. I wondered, what happens after the week is up, and he has his iPad. What will the next carrot dangled in front of him to behave be? Mom and Dad do not embrace the same style of child-rearing, and let me tell you, the boy knows. He plays them against each other and for his own benefit all the time. He had to learn that type of existence, he didn't create it himself. People aren't born that way. What will they be buying him in ten years when he is eighteen? Will he develop an appreciative attitude as he grows older?

Can a young child keep a gratitude journal? Yes! Can a young child help clean out old toys and books and drive them to a children's hospital to donate them? Yes! Can a young child help an elderly neighbor? Yes! Can a young child visit someone who is lonely? Yes! We can look for opportunities at every turn for young children to learn to give of themselves and their time to others. Imagine their smiles as they feel and appreciate gratitude from someone else that they were directly involved in helping.

Personally, I am a strong believer in the written thank you note. Listen, I am on my computer every day. I have an iPhone. I am connected to technology as much as anyone else these days. But I was taught to write a thank you note and taught my daughter to do so as well. So were my nieces and nephew. Now my granddaughters are writing them too. Taking a few moments to express your appreciation and gratitude is a non-negotiable to me.

Our parents were children once too. Most of us learn about parenting from our own parents and/or grandparents. Today's world seems to be so different with the internet ability to communicate anywhere in the world in seconds. We know what is happening on the other side of the world in a flash. I have heard people from my parent's generation say, "I'm glad I'm not raising kids today!" But was it easier in the 60's or 70's? Raising children is one of the most arduous, emotional, and challenging responsibilities we are given on this planet.

Did you know that suppressing your negative emotions can, over time, cause a physical symptom? It's true. If you ignore those emotions long enough, they will emerge physically to get your attention. Your body uses symptoms to alert you when you are out of balance of body, mind, and spirit. Waiting it out, or ignoring an imbalance may result in pain or other health problems. You may not realize how heavy a burden your unresolved negative emotions are to carry around with you. You carry them day and night, and most of the time you may not even be aware of the weight. All of us carry emotional baggage with us to some degree. It might be painful childhood memories, a traumatic car accident or perhaps a fire. Throughout life, we experience loss and grief on a personal level-divorce, death, betrayal, hardship, and failure. The list is long and varies from person to person.

A few years ago, my two sisters and I took a little getaway. We left the kids, husbands, and dogs at home and met at a midway point, which at that time happened to be Asheville, North Carolina. We took in the sights, but spent many hours talking. As we remembered incidents from our childhood, one thing started to become clear. Our perceptions of the same event were so different that it seemed we weren't sisters at all; it seemed more likely we had grown up in different homes! I am the first born so my point of view of particular events differed from my sister who is six years younger. Some incident that was quite painful for one of us was hardly recalled by another. We were truly amazed!

Emotional pain definitely takes a toll on us emotionally and physically. Which do you think is worse: the pain itself or the resistance to it? People tend to fear the pain, fight it, ignore it, run away from it, and ultimately try to bury it. Oprah once described the suppression of emotional pain like trying to hold a huge beach ball under the water. It takes all of your energy and strength to do so, until that moment when you can no longer hold it and it bursts through the surface of the water with a terrific force! How much can you suppress before the tension and effort of doing so will take its toll on your physical body? Doesn't that make sense?

To me it no surprise that my clients feel tired, listless, and in pain. They have low energy levels, and many times suffer from chronic headaches and/or migraines, pain in the lower back and knees, and many have chronic lung and throat problems. Many people have trouble either falling asleep or staying asleep. A lack of rest takes its toll on your home life and work performance. Their medical doctors have run all the typical tests and not found a cause for the problems. They have been on antibiotics, and sometimes been convinced they need to relax or get some sleep with prescription medications. When that doesn't work, or even causes more problems due to side effects. Does any of this sound familiar to you? Do not give up.

Some people choose to ignore the warning signs. They suppress the unresolved negative emotions and think external things will solve all their problems. But a new job, car, house, or relationship, will not fill the void you feel. What you hold on the inside becomes your daily experience of life. I have known people to work toward a goal-an object they desire with all their being. Sometimes the payoff is weeks, months or even years later. They have convinced themselves that when they earn that object their lives will be great. But what is the cost in the meantime? What have they given up while waiting for that to happen? And when they receive it? Disappointment that life isn't like in the movies sets in.

Candace Pert and Bruce Lipton have written books about the chemical reactions in your body from your emotions. Try to think of an emotion as an electrical current coursing through your body and brain. Just like a current, your emotional energies have a frequency too. In your brain you have pathways along which the emotional current travels. The emotion triggers the release of peptides which are chemical proteins that then send messages throughout your body which in turn create a physical response.

Some examples of neuro-peptides that you may know are adrenalin and endorphins, There are others, of course, but the main job of neuro-peptides is to communicate specific responses throughout your body. Endorphins, for example, make you feel good. Your muscles relax, your mood is elevated, your immune system receives a boost, and aches and pains seem to be dampened.

Adrenalin is released when you are frightened, stressed or anxious. If you were ever suddenly startled you might remember feeling that adrenaline surge through your body. That surge was designed to give your body a boost of energy to help you escape from danger.

*"Stress is not necessarily bad for you; it is also the spice of
life, for any emotion, any activity, causes stress."*
~Dr. Hans Selye

Learning how to calm the body and mind are essential. Previously I have discussed some of the many and varied relaxation exercises you can try. One or another may feel right for you. It doesn't matter which technique you try, the end result is to learn how to relax and calm yourself. When I discovered yoga, I learned how to still my mind and breathe. As I lay upon my mat listening to the wonderful voice of my teacher's instructions, I find I cannot think about what I need to do or places I need to go after class. I am totally absorbed in moving my body, holding the poses and breathing. In yoga, prana =life force from the ancient Sanskrit. Your breath is everything.

EXERCISE:

I have used breathing techniques with individuals who have difficulty controlling their angry outbursts. (Think of road rage in adults.) I have taught clients different breathing techniques for helping them relax so they can sleep. It works! Here is one breathing technique that seems to work for people of all ages:

1. Get into a comfortable position. You can sit or lie down. This place should be quiet and without the distraction of phones, TV, radio, etc…
2. You will be inhaling and exhaling through your nose, not your mouth.
3. Now take a few beginning breaths. Breathe in deeply through your nose, hold it for two seconds, and then breathe out through your nose. Do this 2 or 3 times.
4. Next begin to control your breathing by counting to 4 for each inhale. Hold. Then release to the count of four.
5. Repeat this a few times.
6. Then add on to the count-each inhale to the count of six. Hold. Then release to the count of six. Repeat this a few times.
7. Continue adding on the length of each inhale and exhale to eight and then ten. Feel your abdomen rise with each inhale and push the air out with each exhale.

I am sure you will feel relaxed and hopefully you will even fall asleep. Good for you!

In a previous exercise, we did alternate nostril breathing. I have used this technique before and after flying where the air is not pure and clean. The cabin air is recycled and when the plane is on the ground lots of fumes mix in with it. Cabin air is low in humidity and low in oxygen compared to the air on the ground. I only drink water before, during and after a flight.

When you focus on your breath, your mind is cleared from all of its regular chatter. How do you know if what you are thinking is real or just your imagination running away with itself? Eckert Tolle talks about illusion and compulsive thinking. Sometimes when I am ready to sleep my mind seems to take over thinking the same repetitive thoughts and driving myself to wakefulness. The mind struggles for power. That is why focus and clearing the mind through breathing is so powerful.

EXERCISE:

Here is a second technique which works very well before bedtime. I don't remember where I first learned this technique because I have used it for so many years.

1. Lay in your bed on your back. Do not cross your legs. Get comfortable. Lay your hands at your sides with your fingers spread slightly apart.
2. Take a few deep breaths to begin. Breathe in through your nose deeply and exhale through your nose.
3. Place both pinkie fingers down on the mattress and lift all the others. Breathe in slowly and deeply through your nose, hold it for two seconds, then release through your nose.
4. Next lift the pinkies, and place both ring fingers on the mattress. Breathe in slowly and deeply counting to three as you breathe in. Hold for two seconds, and breathe out through your nose to the count of three.
5. Keep going with each successive finger adding to the count. For the middle finger the count is four. The pointer finger's count is five and the thumb is six.
6. Usually you will be breathing slowly and deeply like you do when you are sleeping. This should work. The trick is to concentrate on the breathing and still your mind. When thoughts come up, refocus on the counting of your breaths. Lifting your fingers and changing the count of breaths helps keep you focused too.

Some other things you can do to release suppressed negative emotions are to take a walk barefoot, if possible. Feel the grass between your toes. Connecting with nature helps release negative emotions because you start to breathe and enjoy your surroundings. If you live near the beach, go take a walk. Live near the mountains or woods? Take a hike, literally.

> *"Everything is energy and that's all there is to it. Match the frequency*
> *of the reality you want and you cannot help but get that reality."*
> *~Albert Einstein*

Allow yourself to feel all of the emotions your body and brain offer you. There is no good or bad, right or wrong to your emotions. What you feel is yours and yours alone. Every emotion exists to help you grow and change and learn along your life pathway. Your body, mind and spirit are intertwined. As you go out daily and face the world you are influenced by light, heat, color, movement, sounds, touch and texture, words, actions and more. You are literally bombarded but your brain works with your senses to filter what is important to you at a particular moment in time.

Everything we experience happens for a reason. They create our individuality and uniqueness. No two people are the same or experience a situation in the same way. Even twins in the same place at the same time, internalize and interpret what happens differently. Our experiences are our teachers. It is of the utmost importance that you try to live each and every day in a state of inspiration, creativity, and gratitude. This is not to say to strive for perfection or never have a negative emotion. But be aware of your thoughts. Thoughts become things-your life.

Relationships with family, friends, co-workers, and neighbors are important, but most important of all is your relationship with yourself. Are you one of those people who puts yourself last? Loving yourself is the ultimate gift. There is a little voice in your head that may wonder if that is selfish. Women especially in our society are taught to be nurturers and givers. I think you will be better at nurturing and giving if you take care of yourself too. There will be more to give from a healthier you than from one who is feeling exhausted and drained at the end of the day.

"Self-care is not selfish. You cannot serve from an empty vessel."
~Eleanor Brown

When you learn through your own experiences, you remember those lessons for a long time. I think that is why teenagers tend to ignore their elders. They need to go out and have their own experiences. We only want to protect them and keep them safe from harm, but the lessons we learned may or may not have anything to do with theirs. It is when you face the obstacles, jump the hurdles yourself, and experience the whole process that learning takes place. Coming to a new understanding for yourself based on what you just experienced, is so worthwhile and empowering.

You need to give yourself the gift of time. The journey to change and success begins with small changes that add up over time. You don't have to be a cheetah. Remember the tortoise and the hare? Slow but steady won the race. It is all about making lots of good choices, right choices, for you.

Turtle power! Be a ninja!

CHAPTER SIX

SELF-WORTH

"If you could only sense how important you are to the lives of those you meet; how important you can be to the people you may never dream of."
~ *Fred Rogers*

Have you developed shyness, a fear of speaking up or stepping forward? You look around and everyone else seems to have it all together while you are floundering inside. You might try to blend into the background and suffer silently. I believe your self-worth, or lack of it, is a reaction, a self-preservation, developed over time. What you think, you are. If you think the same negative thoughts about yourself over and over again, it becomes your reality.

When you feel you deserve less than others, jealousy or resentment may follow. These emotions can become all consuming. You can easily fall into a victim mentality. Perhaps setbacks early in life taught you that what seems to come so easily to others is almost impossible for you. When we hold negative emotions inside of us for very long, they build up and we cause ourselves fear and worry over possibilities that may or may not occur. We may tend to focus on anticipating all the possible future outcomes and view them as limiting. In actuality, there is an equal or greater chance of a positive outcome. Feeling less than others prevents you from perceiving those possibilities. Alicia Keys had her musical collaborator point out to her that she used the word "if" a lot. She had never noticed that habit before. Today she uses the word "when" and believes the word "if" should be removed from our language entirely!

The idea of being noticed might even be scary. You blush. You beg off compliments. You can't say no even though you want to. You may do an exemplary job, but wish to be an unsung hero. This can certainly build up resentments if you feel used and abused. Everyone wants to be recognized and appreciated, even those who lack confidence.

Back to the Law of Attraction, what you think of yourself, how you perceive yourself, the self-talk in your head, and how you present yourself to others becomes your reality. The more you focus on negativity the more you attract into your life. When you put yourself down or deflect compliments it isn't modesty or humbleness; you are actually letting everyone know you aren't worthy, even if that is not your intention. Growing up in America, girls especially, are taught to be self-effacing. We don't want to appear conceited or arrogant. But there is a middle ground between the two extremes.

Loving yourself is one of the hardest things for many people to do. We learn to give of ourselves, sometimes thinking 100% isn't enough. It has somewhat to do with the Judeo-Christian work ethic many of us were raised with. When you perceive you have messed up royally, do you treat yourself with compassion and respect? Wouldn't you do that for someone you care about? Why not yourself? Why not be as gentle with yourself as you would be a dear friend? If your friend ever said to you the things you think inside your own head, you would end the friendship.

Louise Hay recommends doing some mirror work on self-love. She says when you wake up, first thing, before brushing your teeth, or starting your routine, look in the mirror. Look into your own eyes. Tell yourself, "I love you. I really, really love you." You will connect with your inner child who may not have heard those words in a long time, if ever. Some of you long for nothing more in the whole world than to have your inner child feel the love it needed and never received. Some of you may have grown up in a household that believed demonstrative loving of a child would spoil him and not prepare him for the realities of the world. I disagree so strongly I shake. I believe that to love and be loved are the most basic needs we all have other than food, air and water.

EXERCISE:
1. In the morning, look in the mirror. Look into your own eyes. Today is a new day. Feel gratitude and love as you gaze deeply into your own eyes. (This might be difficult in the beginning. Usually we look into the mirror to notice wrinkles or dark circles.)
2. Tell yourself how beautiful your eyes are. Tell yourself you are grateful for how well they help you read, do your job, observe your loved ones.
3. Practice.
4. Whenever you feel ready, begin to look into your eyes and talk to yourself with love. Use Louise's words: "I love you. I really, really love you."

5. You can do this every time you stop to check your reflection in a mirror throughout your day. Soon you will be smiling into your own eyes and feel that deep love for yourself. Louise recommends this twice a day but there is no limit!

I recently heard Dana LaMon present as the keynote speaker at a Toastmasters International Conference in Fort Lauderdale, Florida. He had fallen as a young child and became blind by the time he was four. He attended law school and has used his sense of humor to become a champion public speaker. As part of his keynote address he said, "Quality can be controlled and time can be managed, but people must be loved." I jumped to my feet applauding wildly when I heard that, because I do believe that statement to be true. Every person on this planet needs to be loved and to feel loved, especially those that don't think they need it or feel they don't deserve it.

Steve Jobs said, "Your time is limited, so don't waste it living someone else's life. Don't be trapped by dogma-which is living with the results of other people's thinking." Our intuition is a gift. In our culture, we learn at a young age to dismiss it, but to innately understand what our body and mind needs, and to be in touch with those needs, is a treasure. This is the meaning behind being "awakened" and "conscious".

There are as many definitions of success as there are people on the planet. You need to figure out what success would look like and feel like to *you*. Perhaps you seek financial success, spiritual success or emotional success. Is your self-worth intertwined with your looks, your income, or something else outside of you? When you rely on yourself, you feel empowered. You can bring into your life the things you wish, and fulfill your dreams. That has nothing to do with luck. If you fail, or make a mistake, you keep going. You take responsibility for what went wrong and continue to pursue your dreams.

I know some people have had it really rough. It takes a toll. Nothing has been handed to you; you've worked hard in recovery, suffered major setbacks, or lived through loss of close family or friends. You are not alone. If there is one thing I have learned it is that *everybody has a story*. We all carry tales of grief, loss and suffering. Remember, they are just the stories in your head as you have chosen to remember them. If you have been unable to move forward in your life, if you feel "stuck" or victimized, you need to break that old belief pattern. Look in your area for an NET, Reiki or EFT practitioner. They will be able to help you overcome those emotional feelings that have blocked you from being all you want to be and having all you want from your life. After all, this is no dress rehearsal-you get one shot and one shot only. Curtain going up!

I have coached clients who have struggled with the core belief that they were destined to suffer in this life. Their nagging, negative voice says, "You were meant to suffer." I am always astounded when I look into the eyes of someone who believes this. Why would an abundant Universe want to see anyone suffer for a whole lifetime? Well, the answer is--it wouldn't. Somehow, along the way you have limited your own self-worth because you don't believe it is part of who you are. I hope you are willing to do some work around this. Oh, you are! You are reading this book!

Whether you are suffering from physical pain, struggling financially and living paycheck to paycheck, or feeling a lack of appreciation for your hard work and dedication, I personally do NOT believe any of us are here to suffer by destiny or any other means. Quite the opposite-we are all here with the special abilities and traits that make us the only person on the planet just like us! Humans have been blessed with an amazing brain that allows us to think, reason, and FEEL. Sometimes we use it as a weapon to hurt and punish ourselves if we are convinced we are destined to suffer.

Self-worth is what enables us to believe we are capable of using our talents and gifts to live a fulfilling life. You are you. You are the only you on this whole planet of billions of people. Specific gifts are yours and yours alone in the certain combination that makes you as unique as your fingerprints. Max Ehrmann said, "Be gentle with yourself. You are a child of the Universe, no less than the trees and the stars. In the noisy confusion of life, keep peace in your soul."

Our American culture, which is still very much Judeo-Christian based, teaches us that self-love is prideful. When a young child happily declares, "I am the best!" we smile but tell them it isn't polite to speak about ourselves that way. Truly, there is nothing wrong with loving yourself and building your sense of self-worth. How you talk about yourself to others is important, but more important is the truths your own thoughts tell you. Are you acting one way out in public, in the workplace, and going home with negative thoughts telling yourself that you aren't as good as you are telling everyone?

Are you also the person who cannot say no? You set out determined to say no, you tell others you are going to say no, but then when faced with the question, you sheepishly agree and say yes. You cannot possibly feel successful if you are doing things you do *not* want to do. Learn to listen to your true feelings. Don't stifle them, or push them away. They are there to guide you to your best life. When you say yes when you don't want to, you are giving your power away.

Remind yourself that you matter. My daughter loves to write messages to herself on her mirror. Let's face it, all of us look in the mirror. When you write yourself positive messages, they send you off into the world feeling stronger, better about yourself. You can build your self-confidence and your self-worth all at once. I watched a Louise Hay YouTube called "A Conversation with Louise Hay". She has an affirmation that I *love*. When a particular affirmation grabs me, I like to write them down. I carry them in my wallet; sometimes I put a sticky note on the steering wheel, write it on the bathroom mirror, and stick it on the fridge. When you have a problem, stop and say this affirmation:

> *"Everything is happening for my highest good. Out of this*
> *experience only good will come. I am safe."*
> *~Louise Hay*

Take out your notebook and try this exercise.

EXERCISE:

At the top of a sheet of paper write "My talents" Make a list. Keep adding to it. You may start off with just a few, go for a minimum of five. Then as the thoughts roll around in your brain, you will think of more. Keep adding to the list. Think of all the wonderful things others have told you about yourself.

On another sheet, write "My skills". These can range from professional skills to knitting, skiing, or whatever comes to your mind. Keep writing and adding on. Turn the page.

Now write at the top "My Strengths", no weaknesses allowed. Write at least five and then keep adding. If you have someone you trust who really knows you well and you feel stuck, ask them what they would write about you. That might get you going and start building your self-worth immediately.

These lists are works in progress. You can keep adding to them continually. (That's why I like to have my notebook with me at all times.)

You are a complete person and a complete package. Work on replacing what no longer serves you well, and focus on all the great stuff! None of us can go back in time and change the past, but we can certainly be proactive and help shape our own tomorrow!

CHAPTER SEVEN

SELF-ACCEPTANCE

"Owning our story and loving ourselves through that process
is the bravest thing we'll ever do."
~Brene Brown

You need to start where you are, right here, right now, with a new attitude. You are not perfect. No one is perfect. You cannot be the perfect spouse or significant other, employee, or volunteer. It is impossible. If you were striving for perfection, and are still reading this far into the book, you have abandoned that idea by now.

The best case scenario would be unconditional self-acceptance where you embrace all the facets of yourself, what you love and what needs some work. You have terrific strengths. Being aware of, and using what you love and admire about yourself is great, but people who cannot or will not admit they are less than 100% everything may not be as happy as they'd like you to believe.

When you were young, you learned to love and accept yourself to the degree that your parents did. If they disapproved of something you said or did, it created a lasting impression and imprint on your emotional brain. If your parents gave you an overall message of disapproval such as you're a liar, you're not as smart as your brother; you came to regard yourself in this exact way. Your core belief was formed and you took it to be the truth. Who do we hold in higher esteem than our parents when we are little?

To simplify the matter, we learn to parent ourselves the way we were parented. It's what we know. Those core beliefs are from a long time ago. You may not have lived with your parents for a number of years. It is time to revisit what you believe to be true about yourself in terms of your self-worth and self-acceptance.

Your teachers may have done or said something that you remember to this day. Hopefully, you have a very positive message from one teacher that you took as a truth.

For me, it was my 7th grade Spanish teacher, Sra. Rey. To me she was the epitome of everything I ever hoped to be. She was very strict so a lot of the other kids hated her; but I saw a beauty, a grace, a way of connecting with me that influences me to this day. She urged me to be a part of an exchange program even though my family was experiencing financial hardship at the time. I believe my whole life changed from that opportunity to live in Central America and embrace the language, people and culture!

Your level of acceptance, to a degree, determines your level of happiness. Popeye said, "I yam what I yam" which to me indicates that he accepted himself completely. He knew he wasn't perfect, or he wouldn't have to keep fighting Bluto for Olive Oyl. But he ate his spinach, became strong, and took on the world. Now that is confidence.

Every one of us has special talents and gifts that no one else has in the same way. Think about what you are really good at. Every once in a while, I revisit my list that I keep in a notebook. I started by listing the....

Things that Just Come Naturally for Me:

- Organizing
- Prioritizing
- Explaining and teaching
- Reading and learning
- Writing
- Summarizing
- Listing
- Ability to understand, breakdown and teach new information
- Drawing others to me for help
- Responsible and reliable
- Loyal
- Leadership abilities-although many times I prefer to hang back/watch
- I am articulate
- I am intuitive
- I have an artistic eye

You get the point. My list is actually longer and when I revisit it, I add on newly found talents and gifts that I wasn't aware of. For example, I am pretty good now at facing my fears. I used to fear the darkness and being home alone, and they no longer bother me. I love scary roller coasters that make me scream my head off. I love new adventures and wandering off the beaten path.

EXERCISE:

I think this is a good exercise for everyone to try. Open your notebook to a clean page and write your heading "Things That Just Come Naturally for Me".

Understand that the list really never has to end. I have several notebooks I have filled over the years and I save them all. I have the year written in black Sharpie on the front, but they show my personal growth over the years. I have watched my success blossom. I refer back to my notebooks all the time as a resource and as a reminder of where I was and how far I have come.

"Self-acceptance is my refusal to be in an adversarial relationship to myself."
~Nathaniel Brand

In finding self-acceptance, you may need to evaluate the key players in your life. How does my boss speak to me? How do my family and friends talk to me? Is anyone reinforcing my negative self-talk? Am I being belittled or spoken down to? If you answered yes to any of those questions, it is time to reevaluate those individuals. You can't just cut someone out of your life, but you can limit your exposure while you are growing and changing.

Not everyone will be on board with the new you that is emerging. It will make some important people in your life uncomfortable. That is their problem. They are used to interacting with you in a particular way. You may just wind up being a powerful influence on someone else as they watch the changes you make.

Create a support system of like-minded people for yourself. The people who are giving the new you compliments and taking notice of your confidence are the ones to start with. Spend quality time talking and sharing with them. You will be giving yourself a double dose of positivity and a real boost to keep going!

Let's get really clear here for a moment. Self-acceptance does NOT mean giving up your dreams of who you thought you were going to be. That possibility takes place literally every moment. You can create the life and reality you want with your thoughts and actions at any moment at any time. Be kind to yourself. Speak well of yourself in your mind.

EXERCISE:

Visualization of your best self ever!

1. Close your eyes. Take a few relaxing breaths in through your nose and out through your nose.
2. Set your intention to picture the best, highest form of yourself. Picture your life filled with self-acceptance, trust, and abundance.
3. Picture yourself as the best you possible. What do you look like? Add details. Look at your face-are you smiling? Do you like the image you are projecting? Adjust it now. Add what you want and take out what you don't.
4. Study yourself from head to toe. Make adjustments.
5. How are you feeling as you look at yourself? Make adjustments.

This is an exercise that will take time but is so worth it. Repeat as many times as necessary until you begin to feel that shift inside of you.

MENTORSHIP

"I've had a life that has taken many interesting paths. I've learned a lot
from mentors who were instrumental in shaping me,
and I want to share what I've learned."
~ Herbie Hancock

I like to think of mentorship as two people who develop a trusting friendship and work together to help each other grow and change. Personally, since I left home at 15 to be an exchange student, came back to the States and then graduated high school at 17, I have been blessed to find a mentor to look up to in all the places I've lived, studied and worked.

I admit when I was young I thought I knew it all. If you're reading this book, you have stumbled upon the notion that you don't know it all. Neither does anyone. Our work on ourselves is never over. So finding a mentor can be crucial to your success. You can have a professional/career mentor, a personal growth mentor; a mentor can be anyone with whom you develop a close bond and flourish. Spending time with your mentor should be inspiring, leave you wanting more, engage your mind in interesting ways, and be a special time that you look forward to.

In looking for a mentor look for someone you admire and respect. They should be someone you want to emulate. His or her ideas and ethics should mirror yours. Look for the traits in a mentor that you want to embody and embrace in yourself. Those traits are probably already within you, just waiting to be reawakened. After all that is why you admire that person in the first place.

A mentor should be someone with experience and knowledge to share. He or she may be older but it isn't necessary. My mentors when I was young were usually older than me. They had been in my shoes at one time and grown exponentially. I was attracted to their willingness to share with me what they had already learned. A mentorship is based on a friendship. You must be able to know and trust this person because you will be sharing an honest and open relationship.

In choosing a mentor, look for an ally, someone you can trust. This person should be there for you when you need support, to share your successes, and guide you in setting and meeting your goals toward success. He or she is willing to share, open and honest, and even somewhat vulnerable. No mentor is perfect and we have seen some famous people fall when their egos get too big.

In return for the sharing, guidance, and expertise, you must keep an open mind. You are covering territory they have already passed through and if you are open they can save you from common errors or pitfalls, and teach you new ways to negotiate your journey. To go along with this, be willing to compromise. Here is more than one solution to every problem, and your mentor can offer a different perspective on a situation.

Being a good listener can be so hard for some of us. How many of us really listen I mean really listen, rather than wait for the chance to reply? Our brains work so quickly, we need to take a breath and digest not only the words but the facial expression and body language that accompany the words. We are so ready to answer, reply, retort, or correct that sometimes we just miss the point.

Communication is the key! Have you ever had a conversation with someone that led to confusion or conflict? There was a breakdown somewhere, and until it is straightened out there can hurt feelings, loss of a client, or the end of a relationship. Make sure you are both on the same page. One way to do this is to have a clear agenda in mind when meeting with your mentor. That way all of your questions will be answered and you can measure your success between meetings. You will witness your growth and amaze yourself! Another method it to summarize what you heard and match it to what your mentor actually said. You can say something like, "What I am hearing you say is_____." Our past and current emotions filter for us whether we want them to or not. If there is a miscommunication, you both will realize it at that moment and clarify the message.

Your mentor is part of this relationship with some but little reward, so the time you spend with her is time she could be doing other things. Being a mentor is a great experience for the mentor as well as the mentee. Many mentors engage in such a relationship to pay it forward. He was mentored well and wants to pass that along to someone else. We all do have an ego and it gets stroked a bit. Many mentors see themselves as lifelong learners. They are willing to grow and evolve and they do that in part by helping you. Mentorship is a challenge and that could drive some of the relationships as well. Watching someone grow and change, expand their learning and experiences, is rewarding. It is a challenge to see someone take on new experiences that may very well change her life. If you are picked as a mentee, your mentor believes in you! He or she can see your potential beyond what you can see in yourself!

So do your part. You will evolve into a new you and be so glad you did. When you are basking in the rays of your success, you may want to think about paying it forward. How about becoming a mentor to someone else? I have met several people, including my husband, who mentored through the Big Brother/Big Sister program. Eric found it very rewarding to go fishing and boating with his little guy Jason. Our daughter was grown and on her own, and Jason didn't have a dad in his life. They were like two peas in a pod-looking for fun with a dash of mischief!

> *"God did not create you to be alone. He deposited skills,*
> *knowledge, and talents in someone out there who is expected to*
> *mentor you, teach you and encourage you to go high.*
> *Go, get a mentor!"*
> ~ *Israelmore Ayivor*

YOUR THOUGHTS

"Thoughts are boomerangs, returning with precision to their source."
~ Author Unknown

Your thoughts create your own reality. As you step forward to create your own pathway to success, you must realize how powerful your thoughts are.

In our hectic fast paced world it is difficult to make the time to go inside and check what it is going on in there.

Here is an exercise I like to use when I want to reacquaint the thoughts in my head with my feelings, and get in deeper touch with my true self. (Warning: this takes time to develop. Don't give up. Keep trying during different times of day or in different places. Visualization is a powerful tool.)

EXERCISE:

1. Sit comfortably and close your eyes. (If you are not used to this, even just keeping your eyes closed can be a challenge.)
2. Try to focus on your breath and allow the tension you feel to leave your body with each exhale.
3. Think of each inhale as cleansing and clearing your mind and body. Think of each exhale as letting go of worries, doubts, and anxieties.
4. As you feel your breath slow and become rhythmic, imagine a place where you feel very safe. Some people call it "my happy place". For me it is always a place in nature. Sometimes I am at the beach listening to the endless waves, other times I am sitting in a grove of autumn trees. Listen to the sounds of your safe place, breathe in the air and any fragrances, feel the temperature, and keep breathing.
5. Next imagine a tunnel which can be made of whatever appeals to you. For me, I prefer a pathway of trees whose boughs are connected overhead with bits of sunlight breaking through. As you walk, visualize yourself feeling capable and

successful. See yourself strong and confident. See yourself in the "optimal" workplace or in the "optimal" relationship, whatever area you want to gain deeper knowledge of yourself in.

6. Simply open yourself to whatever appears. You may receive some insight or impressions or feelings about the situation. Don't try to push. Just be open and relaxed. You may hear your brain wondering, "Is this real or just my imagination?" Don't listen.

7. Stay in this visualization as long as you can. You will know when you are done.

8. When you are ready, walk back through the tunnel and go back to resting where you started. Keep breathing. Enjoy the feeling of deep relaxation. When you open your eyes, you can record your experience in your journal.

My husband and I like to remind each other to "Think about what you're thinking about when you're thinking about it." So often these days we find ourselves on automatic pilot, we miss out on precious moments of living in the now. We lose focus and cannot even remember what we were thinking. Ever walked into a room and wondered why?

The golden treasure of yourself lies within your fears. I know, that is not how fear feels, fear is scary. But going through the fear and facing it, coming out the other side of it, is where growth takes place. You don't change and grow doing what you have always done. If you can embrace the fear and welcome it into your heart, you can begin to look at and change your thinking. If you really want to make changes in your life, you will have to do something different. You are the author of your life story. Give yourself the permission to stand tall and speak boldly.

Another list I love to make in my journal is:

When My Life is Ideal, I am:

- Paying my bills easily and effortlessly
- Energetic and young
- Traveling first class wherever I go
- Living in a beautiful home overlooking flowing water that I can see and hear
- Recognized for my work in helping others
- Generating multiple streams of income
- Spending quality time with my husband and family
- Teaching others how to heal themselves
- Teaching health to large groups of people

- Living a healthy lifestyle of good nutrition, exercise, prayer and meditation, and restfulness, all with a positive attitude

Many of these have already come to be my life today. They were once just words I had scribbled in my notebook, visualizing, mere thoughts, the life I was working towards. This is just a partial list but I wanted to demonstrate that you can and should put anything and everything you desire on your list. Start your list now-and keep adding on to it.

Khalil Gibran, Persian poet, wrote, "We choose our joys and sorrows long before we experience them."

I LOVE this poem. It was written by Lal Ded, also known as Lalla, a great poet from Kashmir, India from the 14th century:

I was passionate,
    Filled with longing,
        I searched
            Far and wide.

            But the day
                That the Truthful One
                Found me,
                    I was at home.

I prefer not to interpret poems for others, but this one was so important to me. The truth lies within you; there is nothing you can buy in any store anywhere in the world that can take the place of knowing your own truth. The truth is what you have always known, but forgotten. It is still inside of you, you can tap into again. You were lost, but now you're found. There is a deep place inside all of us where we know what we should be doing and when and where and with whom. We doubt ourselves and do what we think is right. But is it right for you? Is an old tape playing in your head telling you what is right even though it isn't serving you well? Erase, erase, erase!

People are living longer lives than ever before. Did you know your body was built to last 120 years? If you knew for sure that you were going to live longer that you ever dreamed possible, have more time than you ever thought as an option, what actions would you take today? We tend to live the first moments in our lives-the first dance, the first kiss, the first date, first job, and so on. We do not ever know what tomorrow, or even the next moment brings. What if we lived as though everyday ordinary moments were the last? Wouldn't that make them more precious? Wouldn't our perspective change?

These are just some ideas for you to think about. Feel free to journal about them in your notebook. There are no correct or incorrect answers, of course. Go by what you *feel*, what resonates with you. If it feels good, or right, then it is. Of course that encompasses only doing what is best for highest good.

YOUR SUCCESS LIST

Let's move on to the good stuff-making positive changes to welcome success into your life with open arms. Spider-Man said, "With great power comes great responsibility." Personally, I prefer, "With great responsibility comes great power." When we are mature enough to take on the responsibility for all we think, do and say, tremendous possibilities begin to appear empowering us with confidence and success.

EXERCISE:

First of all, you need some time to think, a quiet space to work in, a pad and a pen.

1. Start by thinking about what success means to you. For some it is the ability to earn vast amounts of money, for others it might be a well-deserved promotion, or for someone else a lasting and loving relationship.
    What does success mean to you? You will get very clear about this as you start to write. The more clear you are, the more specific, the better.
2. At the top of the paper or pad write the word Success and begin to make a list. You can free write any word or phrase that comes to your mind while thinking about success. Write down any and all ideas. They may seem random, but it might take a while to get the flow going. Try not to judge-write it all down.
3. Take your time with this exercise. You can walk away and come back later to keep adding on. If you see something, read something, hear about something, talk with someone, whatever triggers your interest, simply add it to your list. I don't know about you, but what I love about lists is being able to cross things off. As you achieve success and bring these positive changes into your life, you will scratch them off and continue to empower yourself with even more success and confidence.

What do you want? Power? A promotion? More money? A lot more money? An award? Recognition? Another degree? Finishing something you started long ago and regret not seeing it through? You've got to get really clear about what you want to weed out what you don't want. Where you put your attention is what flourishes. If you concentrate all of your efforts on what is lacking in your life, then that is what you will live. On the other hand, be clear and visualize what you do want more of and that is what will come to you.

<u>Here is part of my original list:</u>

- Nurture and build my relationship with Eric
- Spend quality time with Barbara, Xoe and Xamara
- Live in a state of gratitude
- Appreciate everything I have been and done
- Accept my imperfections
- Try to see myself as my loved ones see me
- Make time to write every day
- Financial freedom
- First class travel
- Recognition at work
- Advocate for children in need
- Deep, lasting friendships
- Meet lots of people with similar interests
- Confidence about how I look
- Ability to speak/give presentations to groups
- Share what I have learned about emotional well being
- Help others transform their lives
- Keep my Facebook business page updated
- Grow my own organic food
- Own a home in the city
- Own a home in the countryside with some land
- Live on the water with spectacular views
- Live in the mountains
- Maintain a healthy lifestyle-this is not a fad
- Keep my web site updated
- Choose positive thoughts
- Manage my stress better through daily meditation
- Pursue more education in everything and anything
- Work for myself helping others

- Multiple streams of income
- Time to meditate
- Be honest with myself
- Embrace the fact that I am different
- Keep swimming upstream when necessary, but look for a path of less resistance without compromising what I believe in
- Tune into the "something" I have that I have not yet been able to name
- Let go of fear at every opportunity presented
- Look for the lesson in challenging experiences
- Go with my gut when I am unsure
- Breathe
- Ground myself
- Get out and network for my business
- Explore studying acupuncture
- Don't take things personally
- Give 100% to what I'm doing when I'm doing it

I did not feel guilty at all writing down what I feel strongly about on my list. I add to it all the time. I carry a notebook with me to collect good ideas, snippets of conversations, interesting words and phrases I come across in my travels. My list is in my notebook. The best news of all is that the list need not ever end. I don't like to think of it as a Bucket List. I simply prefer to think of it as **My Success List**. I am very focused on bringing good into my life.

If you have been unhappy and feeling like a failure for a long time, the bad news is that there is no magic formula or pill that will change that overnight. Sorry. You do not change your failure-success ratio because you read this book or any book for that matter. Now comes the time to find the strength to write your own next chapter.

The very first sentence of this book is, "You already know deep inside why you haven't made all your wishes and dreams come true, because the answer is always inside." I believe this. Your thoughts become your reality. If you think lack, you live lack. If you think failure, you live failure. Somewhere in your mind, you created certain beliefs that you have spent a lifetime believing as a truth. Are they still true for you today? Does it serve you well to hold on tightly to old beliefs? You can replace an old truth with a new one. Why not a new truth of success and happiness?

Right now, you get to become the author of your own story. Right now, from this moment forward you can write the script of your life the way you want your life to be.

A LIFE WITH NO FEAR

FEAR: False Evidence Appearing Real.
~ Author Unknown

Recently my friend and therapist, Larry Dolinsky, asked me what my life would be like if I lived a life with no fear. I stopped, thought for a very long moment before asking, "Is that possible?" He in return asked, "Why not?" as he nodded to me yes. Yes? We can live a life with no fear? That's possible?

I have spent many years facing my fears, fighting the demons in my life's story. My life's story of course is how I have chosen to perceive it and understand it. The story can be rewritten at any time, but the story of my life right now is the one that is in my head that I have accepted. I never thought a life with no fear was within the realm of possibility. I have faced and slaughtered one fear after another, bravely facing each one. I have worked to allay the fears of my inner child. I have worked to find my voice in a positive and assertive way rather than in an angry and aggressive one. But with every fear conquered, another would raise its ugly head, one fear right after another. As soon as I dealt with one, the next test was right there waiting for me.

So how could there be a life with no fear? I couldn't perceive the concept. Larry said, "Fear's biggest lie is that they are limitless." Huh? You mean fear takes over my brain by making me believe it is *part* of the human experience? So what we have experienced in the past, we are conditioned to expect more of the same in the present and future. Have you ever been totally consumed by what "might" happen? You worry about a work presentation, meeting future in-laws, until you can't even sleep at night. That is your brain wrestling with you for power.

"There were many terrible things in my life,
but most of them never happened."
~Michel Eyquem de Montaigne

I must say that as of this writing, I am just beginning to wrap my head around the whole idea. I like it. It intrigues me. I have just started to write that story. That's one of my next projects.

This is one of the lessons I have learned in this physical lifetime. Fear is not real. It feels very real. Some people suffer from panic attacks and/ or anxiety. Fear is ego. Fear is your brain taking over and renting space in your head. Fear is the by-product of the thoughts you create. I am not talking here about danger. Danger is real and your intuition will let you know when you are facing real danger. You must listen. But remember, ___*fear is a choice*___.

EXERCISE:

1. Take out your journal.
2. Think- what would I do if I lived a life with no fear.
3. Write down every single solitary idea, thought, image or vision that comes to mind.
4. When you feel you are done writing, read it over. I guarantee you will have a huge grin on your face!

LEADERSHIP

"If your actions inspire others to dream more, learn more,
do more and become more, you are a leader."
~John Quincy Adams

I recently saw Wayne Dyer as the opening speaker for the Fort Lauderdale I Can Do It! Conference. He said that the #1 regret of people who were dying is- *I wish I would have had the courage to live the life I was destined to live, but I didn't out of fear!*

His advice to all of us-"Don't die with your music still in you."

Do you want to be ordinary? Do you feel a pull, something within you, a purpose, a mission, a feeling that you aren't done with what you came here to do? Yes. That is why you are reading this book. From the beginning of our lives we hear "No!", "Stop!", "Don't do that!" and we are a little more crushed. We grow up with a feeling of limits and lack thinking.

The #1 fear in the world is public speaking. The # 2 fear is death. It has been said that most people would rather be in the box than giving the eulogy! If you are terrified of public speaking, or want to improve your skills, why not look up your local chapter of Toastmasters International. You can be a guest and watch people from all over the world and all walks of life work on becoming better communicators. To find a location near you go to their web site www.toastmasters.org. Not only will you learn how to improve your public speaking skills, you will learn to improve your listening skills. Being a good listener is underrated. As a first time guest, there is usually no cost to attend.

I think it is important to define what a leader is *to you*. Over the years, I have seen many examples of both good leadership styles and bad leadership styles, as I would define it. As an educator, I have learned that motivating others needs to be individualized, but all leadership should stem from kindness. Some people respond to tough love; being told they don't have what it takes has spurred many on to glory. But young or old, many years of experience or fresh and green, I think all people respond best to a leader who is kind, looks them in the eye, and gives them an element of caring.

One of my clients steadfastly held onto some core beliefs that had gotten him stuck on his path to success. "Max" firmly believed that as he had climbed the ranks slowly one rung at a time that everyone should have to do so. He clung to the belief that the higher you went, the less you interacted with those below you. Max would never dream of speaking with anyone outside of his office if he perceived them not to be on his level or above. When he came to me, he was struggling with being "stuck" where he was while others were passing him on the climb to the top.

He took a long hard look at how he defined leadership for himself and then compared that to leaders he had admired throughout his life. We included teachers, religious leaders, neighbors, not just business people. He was able to compile a list of qualities that he felt described good leadership. It was difficult, but then Max rated himself on his effectiveness in using those same qualities that he had admired in others. Our work together then took on changing his leadership style to better fit his new core beliefs.

EXERCISE:

1. Think about all those people in your past that made an impression on you.
2. Write down their names and next to that the words that describe the impression. (Feel free to use lots of adjectives.)
3. Now rate yourself on a simple scale of 1-5 with 1 being not at all or slightly up to 5 being completely satisfied.
4. Rejoice in your high scores of 4-5!
5. Choose one or more of the low scores to work on. Sometimes they are interconnected and you can see where you could easily combine them.
6. Get started. Try! It takes practice and repetition to create a new habit. If it doesn't feel right, or feels too forced, save that one for a later time.

Give yourself a break! Change takes time. The more you rehearse the better it feels. Try talking to the mirror. Make eye contact. Practice your hand shake; not too firm and definitely not too limp. Practice your smile. Some people have trouble with that one. Use the mirror for feedback. Practice introducing yourself.

Everyone should have a brief "elevator speech" that tells people who you are, what you do to help others, and how you differ from your competitors. (By the way it got its name "elevator speech" based on what you could say to a person about yourself or your business during an elevator ride.) The goal is not to "sell" the person, but to entice them to talk more or learn more. Get a business card or contact information for your follow up.

As an example here is my elevator speech:

If you are ready, I can help you feel better. If you are feeling stuck, or like no one is listening to you, I am here to help. We work together as partners to design an individualized program to meet your needs. Through one-on-one sessions, I guide you on the path of healing and self-discovery. This is your opportunity to transform your life.

Here is another, my husband Eric's:

I set up small close-knit networking groups where people get to know, like and trust each other. The ultimate purpose is to exchange qualified business referrals. My average chapter is 15 members which is what separates me from my competition. Your first meeting is free in these one of a kind networking groups.

Here are a few tips that have worked for my clients in the past:

- speak confidently-this goes along with the fake it 'til you make it approach if that is what will help you through
- sit/stand confidently-people read your body language whether doing so consciously or subconsciously
- talk about what you know-then you are your genuine self
- do an honest analysis of your strengths and weaknesses-focus on your strengths
- consider any opportunities that are available-don't automatically say or think "NO!"

EXERCISE:

Write YOUR elevator speech. Practice in front of the mirror. Practice again in front of the mirror. Make eye contact. Smile. Revise it until it sounds like normal everyday conversation. Try it out on a few trusted friends or family members. Revise it again if necessary. Hone it, polish it, memorize it, and USE it.

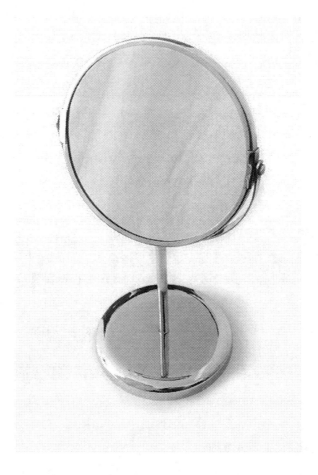

Here is my final exercise for you on making a list – write down the things to do to make you feel alive! Here's my list:

"Things to do to make me feel alive"

- Dressing up
- Listening to a guided meditation
- Looking at old photo albums
- People watching
- Saying a prayer in a sacred space
- Using my iPad to figure out the constellation and planets I see in the night sky
- Checking the moon's progress every night
- Writing a poem
- Baking something
- Inviting people over for a pot luck

- Watching a sunrise or sunset
- Going to the beach during a full moon and sing songs with the word "moon" in them
- Going out in the rain, getting soaking wet, and laughing with sheer joy
- Doing yoga at the beach at dusk, burning incense, and then drinking tea afterwards
- Visiting a museum
- Starting a collection-I collect angels
- Having a coffee with someone I love to be with
- An empty journal with so much potential
- Sitting outside under the stars and watching a campfire
- Listening to beautiful music and being carried away by it
- Yelling "Surprise" when I manage to pull it off
- Bird houses
- Growing my own food
- Floating in a pool or ocean with the sun on my face and cool water beneath me

Those are just a few of mine. My actual list is several pages long. The more you feel alive, the more confidence you will have, and the more success with begin to peek around the corners to find you!

SUREFIRE WAYS TO SUCCESS

I include here a partial list of surefire ways to success. I personally have used every item on this list to boost my success vs. failure ratio. The first time I ever heard the word "Om", I was 15, living in El Salvador, and I thought it to be the most ridiculous concept I had ever heard. (I apologize to Senor Lindo for my reaction at that time.) Thank goodness over time, I became more open minded to learning and experiencing new things, such as meditation.

This list is incomplete. No one or two things work for every person. Based on your previous experiences, you may feel more drawn to one or more, while others will seem impossible right now. As you grow into your feelings of success, you may want to broaden your understanding of your own thoughts and emotions by trying something new. Add to this list on your own as your confidence and success skyrocket.

1. Visualization - So much has been written about the power of visualization that I can't add much. I like to think of it as "Believing is seeing." If you can really see in your mind all that you desire, you will see, little by little, the effects in your life. You can visualize any time, I like to do so during meditation and right before I fall asleep. I let my wishes and dreams stay in my mind all night long by focusing on them before drifting off.

2. Make a vision board_- This is so powerful. I started my first vision board a few years ago. I make a new one as needed. I think about the most important areas in my life: relationships, health, wealth, travel, family time, etc.... I cut out or draw a picture that represents success in that area and glue it on the poster board. I hang it where I can see it all the time.

3. Meditate - Meditation has healing and empowering powers. Taking time to stop the world for a short time and focus inward is energizing and powerful. Meditation helps us emotionally, physically and spiritually to be in tune with our thoughts and feelings. Positive energy moves through your body, mind, and spirit helping you to feel alert and alive and happy.

4. Do yoga_- I Love yoga. (Thank you Val!) Yoga builds strength, flexibility and balance, but also offers an opportunity to honor your breath and focus on the present moment. Better breathing helps you maintain mental calmness, and reduce stress. Yoga helps develop body awareness. I have amazed myself with what my body has been able to do.

5. When facing a fearful situation, picture in your mind the worst case scenario. Anything short of death should help put things into perspective. Then think of the absolute best case scenario. Picture yourself living it, go through the motions in your mind. You can make it happen. Be a possibility thinker. Fear nothing. Life gets better when we can take a risk. Speak up. Go for the promotion. Accept compliments and accolades graciously. All you need do is say, "Thank you."

6. Leave the past behind and move forward. Yes you have made mistakes. We all have. Forgiving yourself is some of the hardest self-work you can do. Accept that the past is over and done and can't be changed no matter how many times you relive and replay it. But your future lies wide open right before you with limitless possibilities for success and happiness. When in doubt, take out your Success List or go look at your vision board.

7. Find a mentor - I am so thankful for the day I met Marlene Cobb Sime. I want to be just like her. She has helped me with my physical and emotional well-being with NET and NAET. She was my inspiration to earn a doctorate so I can do what she does. If you can find someone who brings out your best, and inspires you to challenge yourself, go for it! Only good will come from it.

8. Affirmations - An affirmation is a positive statement written and said in the present tense as if it were already so. Hopefully, as you have been reading this book, you are becoming more aware and conscious of your thoughts. Negatives can be changed into positives. For example "I am going to fail to get that promotion" becomes "I am successful in my work. I receive the promotion I desire."

Affirmations helped change my life. In the past, my first instinct was reactive and negative. I was probably negative 85% of the time. I think I have it down to about 40% and am still working on it. Of course back then I didn't understand the influence my negative thoughts had on my life.

9. Appreciate everything! You have heard about an attitude of gratitude for a reason. It works! Keeping a gratitude journal can help you shift your thinking. Every night before bed, write down at least 5 things you are grateful for and you will see how more and more success flows into your life. At first, you may

only be able to be thankful for waking up. You will see this transform in front of your eyes.

10. YouTube videos- You can watch and listen to all your favorite mentors: Louise Hay, Eckert Tolle, Joyce Meyer, Deepak Chopra, Oprah, Wayne Dyer, Joel Osteen, the list is endless. They are short, sweet and to the point. They are a great way to start your day, and will have you thinking positively all day long.

11. Herbal Teas-Many teas promote emotional and physical well-being. Some will help you relax and sleep, others will help in the prevention of aging. Other teas help cleanse your organs and still others promote and balance digestive wellness. If you do a search on the benefits of herbal teas, you will learn a lot and you can experiment with different types and flavors.

12. Homeopathic Remedies- If you contact the company 1-800-Homeopathy you will learn what you need to know about homeopathy. The father of homeopathy is Samuel Hahnemann based on the doctrine that "like cures like". One of my absolute favorites is Rescue Remedy by Bach. They are flower essences that help you on many levels. Lately I have been hearing advertised on our local radio stations!

NOURISHING YOUR BODY AND BRAIN

The typical American....

Eats fast food at least 2 times per week

Eats out an average of 4-5 times a week

Shops at malls at least once a week

Drinks 3 cups of coffee a day

Drinks 2 carbonated beverages per day

Takes prescription drugs

Is overweight

Eats a donut or muffin for breakfast

Rarely eats dinner as a family

Rushes through a meal

Uses a cell phone during meals-may even sleep with one

Has diabetes

Eats at their desk at work

Buys brand name products

Is easily influenced by advertisements

Lives vicariously through celebrity lives / "reality" TV

Has a high school education

Suffers from at least one addiction

Eats white sugar, white flour products

Eats more packaged food than fresh food

Eats in their car

Doesn't that sound scary? Do you see yourself in there? If you do, try to change one habit at a time. Your brain and body will thank you. Try to add fruits and vegetables to every meal. You can chop veggies to put in an omelet in the morning, or have a smoothie. You can add interesting things to your salad at lunch: sprouts, pomegranate seeds, sunflower or pumpkin seeds, and strawberries or blueberries. At dinner, try adding some new vegetables such as Swiss chard. Make a stir fry with lots of fresh vegetables. Try some Asian vegetables too such as bok choy and water chestnuts. Next picnic or barbecue, bring a huge fruit salad. It is so cool and refreshing on a hot day. Also, if your vegetable list is mainly made up of corn and potatoes, I am sad to report that they work as starches in your body, similar to simple carbohydrates. Sorry.

Try to avoid salad dressings. They are loaded with calories and xenoestrogens (the kind of estrogen no one needs). If they are fat-free, they have sugar and if they are sugar-free they have fat. Something has to give your dressing flavor. My favorite dressing is fresh squeezed lemon (not the juice from the plastic lemon in the produce aisle) and Extra Virgin Olive Oil-first cold pressed. That will have the most flavor and be least processed. You can also use coconut oil or flaxseed oil. I love to sprinkle my salad with oregano and basil and lemon pepper. What a delicious flavor addition!

As for your brain, it is mostly made of fat and water and needs healthy fats to work at its optimum best. The top 10 are:

1. Oysters
2. Whole grains
3. Green tea
4. Eggs
5. Curry
6. Berries
7. Nuts and seeds
8. Leafy green vegetables
9. Oily fish
10. Chocolate - not Hershey bars, raw cacao powder

I was a vegetarian for about ten years, unfortunately an unhealthy one. I felt very strongly about my love for animals and couldn't eat them. The way animals are born, raised, and killed in this country would make me nauseous and weak in the knees. Because I travel often and it can be quite difficult to eat well, I basically supplemented my vegetables with lots of dairy (cheese galore) and grains to feel full. Actually feeling full was a huge problem for me. I NEVER felt full. I was diagnosed with diabetes and put on prescription medication which drove me crazy! You've seen commercials about every drug they are trying to peddle to us: here are beautiful scenes of happy people taking our drug while a quiet voice drones in the background with all of the side effects and reasons why you shouldn't even consider taking this drug for one nano-second!

I am currently following the Paleo Diet. It does include meat but I choose grass fed meats that are organically raised and humanely killed (if that isn't an oxymoron!). Along with giving up dairy, I no longer eat grains, legumes, drink alcohol, or sugar! Fruits and vegetables are organic and I am careful to use high quality oils such as grape seed, olive and coconut. I read every label and nothing comes from a package or container. I am in the kitchen cooking and experimenting a lot! I even make my own paleo mayonnaise. On the Paleo version that I am following the guidelines are very strict, but I have made the decision to go all out and do it 100%. I have never felt better! I am off my medications and my blood glucose levels are normal! I have energy, sleep well, and quite frankly when I look at all the foods I used to eat, I just remember how sick they made me feel. You can do a Google search on paleo and there is tons of information out there. <u>Everyone is different. Please consult with your physician before making major dietary changes. Do the research too.</u> Find out how to be the best and healthiest with whatever food and dietary choices you make.

Herbs such as parsley contain great nutrients: Vitamins A, B, C, and K, and minerals like iron, calcium, folic acid, phosphorous, and manganese. Vegetables contain protein and other essential nutrients as well. Spinach is an excellent source of vitamins K and A, magnesium, folate, manganese, iron, calcium, vitamin C, B12, potassium, B6. Spinach is good for the eyes, is loaded with anti-oxidants, and is an anti-inflammatory. Spinach strengthens the bones, provides protein, phosphorous, vitamin E, zinc, dietary fiber, and copper. It is also a good source of omega-3 fatty acids.

"Your body is on loan to you from God. It houses your soul.
And therefore, it must go back to God.
That's why the body is treated with such dignity and such respect."
~ Athol Ofsowitz

Wouldn't it be nice to gain physical health through eating well? You don't need prescriptions for drugs, when we know we can both prevent and cure disease with proper nutrition. Change your idea of "Pharmacy" to "**Farm**acy"! Personally, I have learned that when I eat lousy, I feel lousy. I have aches and pains. I have difficulty either falling asleep, or staying asleep. I wake feeling tired. You are what you eat. Would you rather pay the doctor or the grocer? Either way you're going to pay!

Here are a few simple rules to follow to make good food decisions:

1. Buy food with thought. I like to have a shopping list. It keeps me focused and I avoid buying things that aren't healthy for me. I read labels on the back not just the front. NEVER shop hungry!
2. I love to cook. I make a joy out of it. I put on music and head to the kitchen to chop and dice.
3. Use less sugar, wheat, and dairy. You will feel the difference.
4. Buy organic, grow your own, or at least buy locally grown foods.
5. Try preparing a weekly menu. Buy what you need. Stick to it. I have a little chalkboard where I write down the meals I am to prepare for the week and then pull out the necessary ingredients when I'm ready.

There is an old Irish proverb, "Laughter is brightest, where food is best." The best foods do not come out of a can, package, box or container. They come from the ground or off a tree. That is my thought when I plan meals, shop and cook.

ON YOUR OWN

You know. Yes, you already know. You have doubted yourself for so long, that the knowing part of you has been quieted and shushed. But it did not disappear. When you are in touch with your innate knowing you feel alive. There is no doubt. There is no negative, nagging voice. You already have everything you need. Our culture can get us tripped up on believing that more is better, and we can easily confuse need with want.

When your heart feels what your mind knows, you are in a state of grace and well-being. You have inner peace and a calmness of body and spirit. Gratitude is a lifestyle and positivity is a choice. One of my favorite sayings is: There is an equal or greater chance of a positive outcome.

I once considered myself a failure, but I was also always a dreamer. I still am. I imagined my life to be better than what it actually was, and now looking back I realize just how many of those dreams did come true. If I can do it, you can too. Some of the people we consider most successful today have seen their share of failure. They grew stronger and never gave up.

Oprah was deemed not appropriate for television. The Beatles were told they had no future in music. Michael Jordan was cut from his high school basketball team. Albert Einstein's teachers felt he would never amount to much.

There are things that you will never understand. Not that you haven't tried. But you need to accept that you have tried your best and accept it for that. Let all else go. You have control over your life only and the choices you make. No matter how much you love and want for others, it really is not up to you. You need to accept that too. Believe in your heart that you are totally surrounded by love, positivity, and everything good life has to offer.

Let go of any old promises you made to yourself throughout your years. The past is past. You can't change it. Wasting time and energy and thoughts anticipating what might come next is draining. Instead, focus yourself on success and positive thinking to bring about the changes you want and desire. What I promised myself at twenty, thirty and even forty no longer seem applicable. I have the new promise of this day and this moment to focus upon.

Recognize the relationship between current limits that you set upon yourself and your future potential. Don't allow self-doubt to stop you from advancing toward success. Overcome your tendency to accept and maintain the status quo, especially if it feels safe. Exult in the experience of looking for new ways to look at and solve old problems. You need to empty out your old patterns so there is room to fill up with new ones.

I love to think of summer thunderstorms. Those storms have vast energy which can refresh a dull situation with new ideas. They roll in with a bluster of wind, and sound and pounding rain. When they leave, everything is washed clean and bright. Success really comes from good energy and enthusiasm. It will spark your creativity and the flow of ideas will fill you up ready to take on the world.

The very first sentence of this book is, "You already know deep inside why you haven't made all your wishes and dreams come true, because the answer is always inside." I believe this. Your thoughts become your reality. If you think lack, you live lack. If you think failure, you live failure. Somewhere in your mind, you created certain beliefs that you have spent a lifetime believing as a truth. Are they still true for you today? Does it serve you well to hold on tightly to old beliefs? You can replace an old truth with a new one. Why not a new truth of success and happiness?

Right now, you get to become the author of your own story. Right now, from this moment forward you can write the script of your life the way you want it to be.

So go ahead. Be a dreamer, a lover of love, a provider of peace. Believe in the majesty of life and honor being all you wish and dream for yourself. Embrace every person and experience on your path in this life. I don't believe in coincidences. Every person comes into your life, or leaves, for your personal growth, if you can see it and accept it on those terms.

I am confident that you are ready to begin this next chapter in your life with more confidence than before. Take baby steps if you need to, or just leap right in. You are the author of your own story. What will you write today?

Namaste.

RESOURCES

(in alphabetical order by topic)

1. Affirmations- Louise Hay www.louisehay.com/affirmations
2. Emotional Freedom Technique-EFT (also known as tapping) www.emofree.com
3. Integrative Healing For All - www.debbiejacobsonphd.com
4. NAET- Nambudripad's Allergy Elimination Technique www.naet.com
5. NET- Neuro Emotional Technique www.netmindbody.com
6. Meditation- this is just one of many resources www.how-to-meditate.org/
7. Toastmasters International www.toastmasters.org
8. Totally Unique Thoughts www.tut.com
9. Reiki - www.reiki.org many resources are available on the web
10. Vision Boards - there are too many web resources so do a search and find one that appeals to you. Beware sites trying to sell you software or items for vision boarding. Keep it simple: pictures and glue.
11. Visualization - too many to choose from, do a search and see what appeals to you
12. Yoga - www.yoga.com is just one resource

SUGGESTED READING LIST

(alphabetical by author)

This list is a sampling only. These authors have written more books than I have included here, but I did include the ones I have personally read. There are many authors out there with the same message; you just have to find the ones that resonate with you.

1. Amen, Daniel G.

   - Change Your Brain, Change Your Life: The Breakthrough Program for Conquering Anxiety, Depression, Obsessiveness, Anger and Impulsiveness
   - Making a Good Brain Great: The Amen Clinic Program for Achieving and Sustaining Optimal Mental Performance

2. Carnegie, Dale

   - How To Make Friends and Influence People

3. Chopra, Deepak

   - Secrets of Meditation: Practical Guide to Inner Peace and Personal Transformation
   - Soul of Leadership, The
   - Super Brain
   - Ultimate Happiness Prescription, The

4. Dispenza, Joe

   - Breaking the Habit of Being Yourself
   - Evolve Your Brain

5. Dooley, Mike

   - Infinite Possibilities: The Art of Living Your Dreams
   - Manifesting Change: It Couldn't Be Easier
   - Notes from the Universe: New Perspectives from an Old Friend

6. Dyer, Wayne

   - Being In Balance
   - Excuses Begone!
   - Power of Intention, The
   - Secrets of an Inspirational Life, The

7. Frankl, Viktor

   - Man's Search for Meaning

8. Hawkins, David

   - Power vs. Force

9. Hay, Louise

   - Heal Your Body A-Z
   - Can Do It: How to Use Affirmations to Change Your Life
   - Love Your Body
   - Meditations to Heal Your Life
   - Power is Within You, The
   - You Can Heal Your Life

10. Hicks, Esther and Jerry

   - Amazing Power of Deliberate Intent, The
   - Ask and It Is Given
   - Law of Attraction, The

11. Hill, Napoleon

- Law of Success, The
- Principles of Personal Power
- Think and Grow Rich

12. Lipton, Bruce

- Biology of Belief, The
- Introduction to Spontaneous Evolution, An

13. Millman, Dan

- Body Mind Mastery
- Everyday Enlightenment
- Life You Were Born to Live, The
- Way of the Peaceful Warrior

14. Murray, Michael T.

- Stress, Anxiety, and Insomnia

15. Pert, Candace

- Everything You Need to Know to Feel Go(o)d
- Molecules of Emotion

16. Sharma, Robin

- Greatness Guide, The
- Monk Who Sold His Ferrari

17. Sauget, Linda

- If You Think It

18. Tolle, Eckert

- New Earth, A
- Power of Now, The

19. Williamson, Marianne

- Age of Miracles
- Return to Love, A

20. Ziglar, Zig

- Better Than Good
- See You at the Top

WORKS CITED

http://www.publicdomainpictures.net/view-image.
php?image=57168&picture=heart-of-candles

http://www.publicdomainpictures.net/view-image.
php?image=42720&picture=growth-chart

http://www.publicdomainpictures.net/view-image.
php?image=56853&picture=magnet-illustration

http://www.publicdomainpictures.net/view-image.
php?image=37076&picture=turtle-doodle

http://www.publicdomainpictures.net/view-image.
php?image=31234&picture=love-message-2

http://www.publicdomainpictures.net/view-image.
php?image=19481&picture=making-change

http://www.publicdomainpictures.net/view-image.
php?image=76557&picture=compass-silhouette

http://www.publicdomainpictures.net/view-image.
php?image=2562&picture=face-the-monster&large=1

http://www.publicdomainpictures.net/view-image.
php?image=51939&picture=mirror

ABOUT THE AUTHOR

Debbie Jacobson is a native New Yorker. She has lived in El Salvador, Guatemala, Mexico, Arizona and Florida but has somehow managed to keep the Brooklyn accent with slightly nasal undertones. Her Spanish accent is pretty darn good. One of her favorite pastimes is seeing the look on people's faces when she begins a fluent conversation in Spanish.

Blessed with a most understanding and supportive husband, Eric, she lives in Tamarac, Florida. Bella, an 8 pound rescue Yorkie-Poo also runs the household. Daughter Barbara, and granddaughters Xoe and Xamara have all expanded her heart as wide as the Universe.

Interestingly, Debbie has a B.S. in Business Administration, and an M.A. in Education and has been teaching 28 years, so far. She decided to go for a doctorate in Holistic Nutrition and received her Ph.D. in December, 2009. She has studied the Emotional Freedom Technique, the Neuro Emotional Technique, Nambudripad's Allergy Elimination Technique, and Reiki with certification I and II. She has recently been mesmerized by Doreen Virtue and studying angels.

Debbie is working with clients to help them transform their lives, considering herself to be the guide on the side as she educates, motivates, and inspires others on their journey of healing body, mind, and spirit.

Her personal journey has been long and full of lessons. <u>Create Your Own Pathway to Success</u> is her second published book. Her first book is a cookbook entitled <u>Cooking For Dormies.</u> It is dedicated to students of all ages who would prefer to make healthy choices while expanding their brains. Book three is already started and is about reversing Type II Diabetes.